Louise D. Speer

Valuable and tried Receipts

Louise D. Speer

Valuable and tried Receipts

ISBN/EAN: 9783743327221

Manufactured in Europe, USA, Canada, Australia, Japa

Cover: Foto ©Lupo / pixelio.de

Manufactured and distributed by brebook publishing software (www.brebook.com)

Louise D. Speer

Valuable and tried Receipts

VALUABLE AND TRIED

RECEIPTS

COLLECTED BY
LOUISE D. SPEER

PITTSBURG
STEVENSON & FOSTER COMPANY
MDCCCXCVIII

PREFACE.

IN collecting these receipts—to be sold for Charity—care has been taken to use none that have not been tried and found satisfactory. As far as possible, the names of those who have given the receipts are attached to them; but in some cases these names will be unfamiliar, as many of the receipts are very old ones. A part of those having no names attached are old family receipts, which will be found very useful and valuable.

L. D. S.

ABBREVIATIONS USED.

.... professional.
.... peck.
..... gallon.
.... pound.
... ounce.
.... quart.
. ... pint.
.... cup.
. tablespoonful.
..... teaspoonful.
..... saltspoonful.
.... hour.
.... minute.

EQUIVALENTS OF WEIGHTS IN MEASURE.

One rounded tbsp. butter, ... 1 oz.
One rounded tbsp. granulated sugar . . . . 1 oz.
One heaping tbsp. powdered sugar . . . . . 1 oz.
Two rounding tbsp. flour . . . . . . 1 oz.
Two rounding tbsp. ground spice . . . . 1 oz.
Five medium sized nutmegs . . . . 1 oz.
One qt. sifted pastry flour . . . . 1 lb.
One qt. sifted new process flour, less one gill . . . . . . 1 lb.
One pt. granulated sugar . . . . 1 lb.
One pt. butter, packed solid . . . . 1 lb.
One pt. ordinary liquid . . . . 1 lb.
One solid pt. chopped meat . . . . 1 lb
One c. rice . . . . ½ lb.
One c. Indian meal . . . . 6 oz.
One c. stemmed raisins . . . . 6 oz.
One c. cleaned and dried English currants . . . . 6 oz.
One c. grated bread crumbs . . . . 2 oz.

In case you wish to find the fractional parts of a cupful, to make a small quantity of anything, you will find the following table useful. The cup referred to is the common kitchen cup which holds half a pt.

Eight rounding tbsp. flour . . . . 1 c.
Eight rounding tbsp. sugar . . . . 1 c.
Eight rounding tbsp. butter . . . . 1 c.
Sixteen tbsp. liquid . . . . 1 c.
Two gills . . . . 1 c.
A common tumblerful . . . . 1 c.

SOUPS.

CLEAR SOUP.

One soup bone and three lbs. of meat put on to boil with one c. tomatoes, one carrot, celery, tops and all, parsley, salt, pepper, bay leaf and two onions with seven or eight cloves stuck in each one. Simmer all day—strain, cool, and skim off grease. Next day clear with whites of eggs and shells. *Lucy Gray, Pro.*

CLAM SOUP.

One qt. clams, one onion, parsley, celery, red pepper, one pt. milk, yolks of two eggs, one tbsp. flour not heaping and two tbsp. butter.

Put the clams on to boil with the onion, parsley, celery, red pepper and salt. Boil an h. or more. Cream flour and butter and add to clams. Strain out the clams and add to the stock the milk, which has been whipped. Eggs to be beaten in the last thing.

Mrs. H. L. Johnston.

OKRA SOUP.

Shin of beef or knuckle of veal is best, one-fourth pk. tomatoes, one-fourth pk. okra, two onions, bunch of herbs, one grain whole allspice, pepper and salt. The soup must be boiled eight or nine h., strained through a colander. Good to make it the day before using. Skim off all grease. One-half doz. hard crabs are a great improvement.   *Mrs. J. L. Johnston.*

CALF'S HEAD SOUP.

Boil a calf's head in two gals. of water. When boiled enough remove it from the pot, and bone; reserving the brains and tongue for force meat. Cut all the rest into small pieces and season to taste with red and black pepper, salt, a little onion, parsley, thyme, sweet marjoram, mace, cloves, allspice and nutmeg. Strain the liquor and put the meat in it, allowing them to boil together well. Then chop fine the tongue and brains, season to taste, make into balls, using a raw egg, and fry. When the soup boils and is nearly done add these balls with a tumblerful of wine. Put chopped hard boiled egg in soup tureen before serving.   *Miss Jennie McC. Taylor.*

OX TAIL SOUP.

Take two ox tails and fry until brown with two onions and two tbsp. of butter. When brown add four qts. of water and two carrots, cut up fine and boil for three h. When boiled set aside to cool, and when cold skim fat off top and put into a skillet with two tbsp. of flour and stir until brown, then add one qt. of stock and turn back into rest of soup. In the meantime cut the meat off the ox tails into small pieces and place in the bottom of tureen. When the soup is ready to serve add one-fourth tsp. of curry powder and three tbsp. of sherry.
   Mrs. Geo. C. Burgwin.

SOUPS.

CHICKEN CURRY WITH RICE.

Two qts. chicken stock, one slice of onion, one stalk of celery, one-half c. cooked rice, one tbsp. of butter, one-half tsp. curry powder. Boil slowly for thirty m. the stock, onion and celery. Strain and add curry powder, rice, butter, salt and pepper to taste. Let it come to a boil.

This may be served in bouillon cups. If desired creamy, add one tbsp. of flour and one c. of cream.

John T. Writt.

TURKEY SOUP.

After cutting from the remains of a turkey as much fat as possible, break the bones and put them into the soup pot, together with any dressing and bits of tough meat left from a turkey dinner; cover with three qts. of cold water and simmer for four h.; after the soup has been cooking for one h. add one-third of a c. of rice; after three h. remove the bones and skim off all the fat. Put three tbsp. of butter into a small frying pan and when melted put into it an onion and two stalks of celery cut fine; cook slowly for twenty m.; then skim the vegetables from the butter and put them into the soup. Into the butter remaining in the pan put two tbsp. of flour, add this to soup and after cooking ten m., season with salt and pepper to taste. Strain through sieve and serve.

Emma Piper, Pro.

BEEF TEA.

Take one lb. of beef, cut into very small pieces. Carefully take all the fat from it, put it into one qt. of cold water, and boil it down to a pt. Strain it and add a little salt.

SOUPS.

Take one tbsp. of arrowroot and three tbsp. of sweet cream. Beat them together until very light. Let the tea come to boiling heat, then stir in the cream and arrowroot, but don't let it boil afterwards.

Mrs. Brickhead.

MUTTON BROTH.

Nine lbs. mutton, all lean meat. Put it into a vessel with five qts. cold water and add one carrot, chopped fine, one onion and a bunch of parsley. Let simmer all day and add another qt. of water if necessary. This should be jellied when cold. Skim off the fat, season with salt, and reheat when you wish to use the broth.

Mrs. McClintock.

CHESTNUT SOUP.

Remove the outer peel from twenty-five Italian chestnuts; pour scalding water over them and rub off the inner coating. Put them into a saucepan with one qt. soup stock and boil three-quarters of an h., drain, rub them through a colander, then through a sieve or pound to a paste. Season with salt and pepper, add gradually the stock in which they were boiled, then add extra pt. of stock; boil once and draw to one side of fire. Beat up yolks of two raw eggs, add them to one qt. warm milk, whisk the milk into the soup, taste for seasoning; pour into a hot tureen and send to the table with croutons.

CORN SOUP.

One can cornlet or corn, one pt. cold water, one qt. heated milk, two tbsp. butter, one tbsp. chopped onion, one and one-half tbsp. flour, two tsp. salt, one-fourth tsp. white pepper, yolks of two eggs.

SOUPS.

Chop the corn and cook it in cold water twenty m. Melt the butter and add the chopped onion, and cook till light brown. Add flour and when thoroughly mixed add milk gradually. Add mixture to corn and season with salt and pepper. Rub through sieve. Heat again. Beat yolks of eggs, put them in soup tureen and pour soup over them slowly. Serve as soon as mixed.

RICE AND TOMATO SOUP.

One can of tomatoes, one-third of a c. of rice, a large onion, a qt. of water, three tbsp. of butter, three tsp. of salt, half a tsp. of pepper and two tbsp. of flour. Cook tomatoes and water together; brown the onion in the butter, then skim the onion from the butter and add to the tomatoes and water ; put the flour with the butter remaining in the pan and cook until smooth and frothy, then add the other ingredients. After simmering slowly for half an h. strain over the rice, add seasoning and cook slowly for an h. Stir occasionally to prevent the rice from sticking to the bottom of the kettle. Serve very hot. *Mrs. H. S. Denny.*

RICE SOUP.

Two qts. of any kind of stock ; heat and skim ; then add half a c. of rice which has previously been cooked in a little milk; add seasoning to taste ; simmer fifteen m. and serve. *Mrs. H. S. Denny.*

GREEN CORN AND TOMATO SOUP.

Three pts. of stock, a qt. of sliced tomatoes, a qt. of corn sliced from the cob, one tbsp. of butter and one of flour ; salt and pepper to taste. Cook stock, tomatoes and corn cobs together for half an h. ; then strain into another kettle and add the corn, the flour and butter mixed together and enough salt and pepper to season well. One tsp. of Worcestershire sauce is a great improvement. Cook forty m. *Emma Piper, Pro.*

GREEN PEA SOUP.

One can of peas, a qt. of chicken stock, a c. of cream or milk, two tbsp. of butter, two tbsp. of flour, one onion. Salt and pepper to taste. Cook onion, peas and stock together for twenty m.; then remove the onion and rub the peas and stock through a sieve; return the soup to the kettle and let it simmer for ten m.; rub the butter and flour to a cream and gradually add to this half a c. of the soup; then pour all together and add pepper, salt and cream and boil three m. *Emma Piper, Pro.*

GREEN PEA SOUP.

Take a qt. of shelled peas and two qts. of water, boil the peas until soft then mash through a colander until all the pulp has passed through; then throw away the skins, and return the pot to the fire. There must be a piece of meat boiled with the peas, either a piece of middling the size of your hand or a shin of cold cooked veal or lamb. Season with salt, pepper and a bunch of thyme, parsley, and mint, which must be taken out when soup is dished. Thicken with a little flour, egg and milk as you would do chicken soup.

MARROW BALLS.

Mix well together one-half c. finely chopped beef marrow, one c. sifted flour and one-fourth tsp. salt. Wet with sufficient ice water to form a stiff paste. Form into tiny balls the size of a marble, drop into boiling hot soup, cover closely and simmer for fifteen m. just before serving the soup.

SOUPS.

SOUPS.

SOUPS.

FISH AND SAUCES.

FRICASSEE OYSTERS.

Take two oz. of butter and brown in a stew-pan. Having wiped the oysters dry, put in the butter with salt and pepper to taste. When the oysters are hot, mix in a tbsp. flour and a good piece of butter. When these have been cooked, stir in the yolks of three eggs.

Mrs. H. L. Johnston.

OYSTERS ON THE CHAFING DISH.

Have a dozen large, fresh, salt water oysters. Open them over the chafing dish so that none of the juice escapes. Season with black pepper, red pepper, one tsp. Worcestershire sauce, a very little salt, a generous lump of the best butter and a large glass of good Sherry wine. After this is all in the chafing dish light the lamp and when it is thoroughly heated through and simmers, it is done. The oysters should look plump when cooked enough.

OYSTERS A LA NEWBURG.

For this dish purchase a half lb. of little scalloped crackers, for the effect rather than for the cracker. Do not have them sweetened, of course. Put twenty-five

FISH AND SAUCES.

oysters over the fire in their own liquor. Stir carefully until they come to a boiling point. Drain carefully. Put two tbsp. of butter into a frying pan; add a tbsp. of flour; mix. Add a gill of cream or milk (cream preferable), and when boiling add the yolks of two eggs and the oysters. Bring again to boiling point; season, and turn into a dish. Sprinkle over two tbsp. of sherry, and put the little crackers all around the dish as a garnish. Serve immediately.

PANNED OYSTERS.

To twenty-five oysters take piece of butter size of an egg. Bring it to the boil in a frying skillet. Wipe but do not wash oysters and place them in the butter with two small pieces of mace. Season to taste with salt, black and red pepper or tobasco sauce. In panning oysters they should be turned constantly and never placed on top of each other. *L. W. Washington.*

LITTLE PIGS IN BLANKETS.

Season large oysters with salt and pepper; cut fat bacon in very thin slices and wrap an oyster in each slice and fasten with a wooden toothpick. Heat a frying pan and put in the little pigs. Cook just long enough to crisp bacon, about two m. Place on slices of toast, cut in small pieces. Do not remove skewers. Garnish with parsley. Have the pan very hot before the pigs are put in and shake continually, do not burn.

Josephine Frank.

SOFT CRABS.

Kill and clean them. Flour and fry them like chickens. Make a little cream gravy and put under them.

Mrs. H. L. Johnston.

FISH AND SAUCES.

LOBSTER A LA NEWBURG.

The meat of three good sized lobsters cut in pieces—not too small—over which pour half a tumbler of sherry wine, allowing it to stand one h. Beat twelve eggs light. Heat one qt. cream in double boiler, add eggs, stirring constantly until it is the consistency of custard; add a little mace, cayenne pepper and salt. Pour this sauce *hot* over the lobster and serve. It is best to keep the lobster and wine over steam while preparing the sauce. One-half this quantity will serve five people.

Mrs. Wm. A. Thompson.

SHAD ROE.

Soak half an h. in salt water cold, then rinse in cold water and put on to cook with just enough water to cover it, one small onion, a few sprigs of parsley, a piece of celery, salt and a shake of red pepper. Boil half an h. covered. After boiling, mash, add a little milk, one tsp. of Worcestershire sauce, a small piece of butter creamed with a tsp. of flour. Last add the yolk of an egg.

Mrs. H. L. Johnston.

SHAD CUTLETS.

Boil a shad, also the roe. Pick out all the bones, cut up and mix with cream sauce, with the addition of the yolks of two eggs. Season with salt, pepper, sherry wine, parsley and Worcestershire sauce. Stir this all together—barely thick enough to mould into cutlets and set out to cool. When ready to serve form into cutlets, dip into egg and bread crumbs and fry in deep lard.

Emma Parker, Pro.

FISH AND SAUCES.

HALIBUT A LA CREME

Two or three lbs. of halibut, one qt. milk, one teacup flour, two small onions, one-fourth lb. butter, nutmeg, salt, pepper, bread crumbs. Boil halibut in water into which salt has been thrown. When done flake in fine flakes from the bones, put the milk and onion chopped fine in stew pan. Let milk come to boil, add flour made smooth with little cold water and seasoning, stir until it thickens, add butter, strain through sieve.

Put some of the mixture into dish in which it is to be served, then put alternate layers of fish and sauce, finishing with the sauce on top. Cover with bread crumbs and place in oven to brown. A little wine added to the seasoning is an improvement.

ROCK FISH A LA CREME.

Take a rock fish and rub it well with salt, put it into a kettle with enough water to cover it. As soon as it boils put it at one side where it will just simmer. Let it stand one h., then draw all its bones. Put one oz. of flour in a saucepan to which add gradually one qt. of cream, mixing it very smoothly, then add the juice of one lemon, one onion chopped fine, parsley, nutmeg, salt and pepper. Put this on fire until it forms thick sauce, stir in quarter lb. butter, strain through sieve, put a little on serving platter, then lay the fish on platter and turn the sauce over it. Beat to a froth the whites of six eggs and spread over the whole, set in oven and bake one-half h. Be careful to bake only light brown, nice without eggs but not so handsome.

FISH AND SAUCES.

FISH A LA CREME.

Boil a fish weighing four pounds in salted water (white or blue fish are best). When done remove skin and bones. Boil one qt. of rich milk. Mix butter size of an egg with three tbsp. of flour and stir it smoothly into the milk, adding, also, two or three sprigs of parsley and half an onion minced fine, a little cayenne pepper and salt; stir until it has thickened. Butter a baking dish. Put in alternate layers of fish and dressing, having the dressing on top; sprinkle with bread crumbs and bake half an h. Garnish with parsley and slices of hard boiled egg. *Mrs. H. S. Denny.*

FISH BALLS.

Mix with one c. of mashed potatoes (unseasoned), one-half c. of shredded codfish; add to this two eggs and a pinch of pepper, beating all until light and creamy. Shape, roll in beaten egg, which has a tbsp. of milk added to it; then in cracker meal; drop in boiling fat and fry to a light brown. Drain on brown paper.

Emma Piper, Pro.

DRESSED SALMON WITH SAUCE.

One can salmon, two eggs, two tbsp. butter, one-half c. bread crumbs, minced parsley and salt and pepper to taste. Mix the butter through the salmon, add seasoning and bread crumbs and mix thoroughly with the fish. Beat the eggs and add them last. Turn the whole mixture into a well buttered mould and place in the steamer. Steam for three quarters of an h., then place the mould in cold water for a few m. and turn out on the dish on which it is to be served.

SAUCE.—One tbsp. butter, one tbsp. corn starch, one c. milk, yolk of an egg, juice of a lemon. Salt and red pepper to taste. Mix same as cream sauce.

ROLLS, MUFFINS, ETC.

BOSTON BROWN BREAD.

One c. yellow corn meal, two c. rye meal, one-half c. molasses. Even tsp. soda dissolved in boiling water, and stirred in molasses. Three c. milk, even tsp. salt. Steam two and one-half h. *Mrs. William Sturgis.*

ROLLS.

Three qts. flour, one large tbsp. lard, one tsp. salt, handful sugar, one qt. night's milk, warm, one cake compressed yeast.

To mix rolls—at night—one qt. flour, lard, one-half the milk, salt and sugar are to be mixed together. Add the rest of the milk with the yeast dissolved in it, and beat hard. Work hard with the hands, and set in a warm place to rise. Work in the morning two h. before breakfast, and put in roll pans to rise till time to bake for breakfast. *Mrs. George A. Castleman.*

POTATO ROLLS.

Two large potatoes boiled in one qt. water, two qts. flour, one cake compressed yeast dissolved in one-half c. luke warm water, mix potato water and yeast and set in flour at nine in morning. Work into stiff dough at noon

ROLLS, MUFFINS, ETC.

and add one tbsp. lard, one handful sugar, one tsp. salt. Let it rise until four o'clock when it should be kneaded slightly and rolled out. Cut in rounds about an inch thick. Dip in melted butter, fold over and bake in time for supper. *Mrs. George A. Castleman.*

POTATO ROLLS.

Pare, boil and mash five large potatoes, then add butter, size of an egg, one tbsp. of sugar, one tsp. of salt, yolk of one egg, one c. of warm milk, one c. of yeast and in it dissolve one-half tsp. of soda. Flour enough to make stiff batter. Make them in the morning about 10 o'clock if you wish them for tea. Let them rise until time to make into rolls. We bake ours in muffin pans.

Mrs. Albert H. Childs.

TURN OVERS.

One egg, one qt. flour, one tbsp. lard, one gill or one-half cake yeast, mix with warm water. Let rise over night. Roll out thin and cut with a tumbler, let rise one h., double over and bake quickly.

Mrs. J. B. Washington.

RUSK.

One pt. new milk, one small c. yeast, flour enough to make soft batter. This is to be set at night, with the flour stirred in with a knife.

In the morning stir in one c. sugar, three eggs beaten separately, one tsp. salt, piece of butter the size of an egg. Then stir in one pt. flour and let rise till light. Work into small cakes, let rise again and bake in quick oven. *"Friendship Hill."*

ROLLS, MUFFINS, ETC.

RUSK.

Two qts. flour, three eggs beaten very light and separately, milk and butter warmed. Enough to make them rich with butter and soft with milk, two full c. of white sugar, yeast, nothing outside. Make them out and let them rise very, *very* light before baking; they can scarcely be too light. Bake tolerably quickly. Make about noon and let rise until 9 or 10 in the evening; then put them in the pans and let them rise all night, and bake in the morning. They must not be left in too hot a place—kitchen, away from the fire.

Miss Mary Johnston.

GRITS MUFFINS.

Nice for breakfast. Two c. grits boiled until soft, four eggs beaten separately, one tbsp. butter and one-half tbsp. lard stirred into the grits while warm, one pt. corn meal and one qt. milk. The whites of the eggs are to be added last. The muffins must be baked and served in little china cups, or skillets.

Mrs. Walter Smith.

HERMITAGE MUFFINS.

One pt. of flour, one pt. of milk, two eggs and a pinch of salt. The eggs should be beaten separately and very light, and the oven should be very hot.

Mrs. Geo. C. Burgwin.

BROWN FLOUR MUFFINS.

The point is *no eggs*. One qt. milk, two tbsp. of yeast, enough brown flour to make a thin batter, one small c. of brown sugar, lump of butter; baked in little cups, and, if made well, *so light and wholesome.*

Mrs. J. L. Johnston.

ROLLS, MUFFINS, ETC.

ENGLISH MUFFINS.

This recipe makes two doz. muffins.—Two qts. flour, two large potatoes, one qt. water that potatoes are boiled in, one cake compressed yeast, one cooking-spoonful lard, two tbsp. sugar dissolved in potato water. Mash potatoes in water (one qt. when boiled) strain through sieve and use to mix dough—not quite as stiff as bread dough. Mix smoothly, do not work, and set over night. In morning work out on board and roll one-half inch thick with rolling pin. Cut with good sized biscuit cutter and let rise for one and one-half or two h. Slightly grease griddle and bake light brown on both sides. Put in drip pan and set in warm place to dry. Butter before serving. These muffins may also be toasted on both sides, split and buttered. They will be found even nicer done this way than when fresh. *Miss Lulu G. Riach.*

SHERWOOD BISCUIT.

One pt. flour, one tbsp. yeast, and water to make a sponge as for bread. When light work into the sponge one qt. flour, one tbsp. lard, one pt. buttermilk, in which a pinch of soda has been dissolved. Work well for ten m. and make into small biscuit with the hands.
Mrs. J. B. Washington.

EGG PONE.

One-half pt. corn meal, one-half pt. flour, sift together, six eggs, two tbsp. butter and two tbsp. lard melted together, one qt. morning's milk. *Mrs. J. L. D. Speer.*

CORN BREAD.

One-half c. rice put to soak over night. Boil in the morning till soft. Then add two c. white corn meal, one

ROLLS, MUFFINS, ETC.

heaping tbsp. butter and lard mixed, one egg beaten separately, milk enough to form soft batter, a little salt and last one tbsp. baking powder.

DELICIOUS CORN BREAD.

One qt. corn meal, scalded with one pt. boiling water; add to this one pt. sweet milk, stir to a smooth batter, drop a large cooking spoonful at a time on your hot griddle in separate cakes, let it stand to get lower crust well started, and then place the griddle in hot oven on the top grate, and let bake about half h.

CORN MUFFINS.

One c. flour, one-half c. corn meal, one and one-half tsp. baking powder, one-fourth c. sugar (or less), one-half tsp. salt, one egg, one c. milk, one tbsp. butter. This recipe makes one doz. muffins. Grease muffin pans before mixing the muffins. Thoroughly mix and sift together the dry ingredients. Beat the eggs whole and add the milk. Add the milk and eggs to the dry ingredients and lastly thoroughly mix in the melted butter. Bake in moderate oven for twenty m.

DROP BISCUIT.

For a family of three, take two c. flour, two large tsp. Royal baking powder, small pinch of salt, sift all together and stir in as much sweet milk or cream as will make it as stiff as can be stirred, drop on greased tins and bake in a quick oven. *Mrs. Nancy Frank.*

BAKING POWDER BISCUIT.

One pt. flour, two tsp. baking powder, one-half tsp. salt, scant c. milk or water, one tbsp. butter or lard. Sift

ROLLS, MUFFINS, ETC.

flour, baking powder and salt together and work the fat into the flour with the finger tips. Shape the dough with the hands and cut out with small biscuit cutter. Bake from twelve to fifteen m. in a quick oven.

"MARGARET'S" SCOTCH SHORT-BREAD.

One lb. of flour, one-half lb. butter, one-fourth lb. sugar. Cream the butter, stir in the flour and sugar gradually. Made out on a board with the hand in square cakes. Stick it very well with a fork. Bake on tin sheets in an oven moderately heated.

Mrs. H. L. Johnston.

WAFERS.

One qt. wheat flour, one pt. of milk, a heaping tbsp. of melted butter, mixed. Thin the batter with water to the consistency of flannel cakes. Bake in a wafer iron. About a tbsp. of batter to each wafer. This is the full recipe, but it is not necessary to make the full quantity at once. Half is about what one needs at a time. *Mrs. (Dr.) Tom Murdoch.*

SODA CRACKERS.

One qt. flour, one tbsp. butter, one-half tsp. soda, one tsp. cream of tartar. Mix well, roll thin and bake immediately. *Mrs. J. B. Washington.*

MARYLAND BISCUIT.

One qt. flour, one light tsp. salt, piece of lard the size of an egg. Mix with *ice* water to a rather stiff dough. Beat with meat beater until the dough is well blistered.

Make into biscuit by hand, pressing until thin. Biscuit must be stuck with fork. Bake in moderate oven for twenty minutes. *Mrs. J. B. Washington.*

POP-OVERS.

Two c. of milk, two c. of flour, three eggs, one-half tsp. of salt. Grease the pan, and put in oven to get very hot. Beat the eggs, without separating them, until very light; add to them the milk and salt. Then pour this gradually on the flour, stirring all the while. Do not add too rapidly or the batter will be so liquid that it cannot be beaten smooth. Strain through a sieve to remove any little lumps which may remain. Take the pans from the oven, fill them half full with the batter, put them in a quick oven and bake about twenty-five minutes. They should swell four times their bulk. The pans in which these Pop-Overs should be baked can be gotten at Horne's. *Mrs. Horace G. Dravo.*

BUTTERMILK CAKES.

One qt. buttermilk, one tsp. salt, one egg, one tsp. soda or saleratus, flour to make soft batter. Beat the egg, add to it the buttermilk; add salt and mix well. Dissolve soda or saleratus in two tbsp. boiling water, then stir into the buttermilk and add the flour gradually, stirring all the while, until you have a batter that pours smoothly from the spoon. Give a good beating and bake quickly on a hot griddle.

BREAD CAKE.

Take a piece of raised bread-dough large enough for one loaf; mix into it, one tbsp. butter, one c. sugar, one

c. raisins, and one of currants, one-half tsp. each of cinnamon, cloves and allspice, let rise, which will take some time, and bake as bread.

BUCKWHEAT CAKES.

Into a deep pail or pan put one pt. of buckwheat, a c. of Indian meal, a tsp. salt, and one-half c. of liquid yeast; add to this a little more than a pint of warm water, and a tbsp. of molasses; beat the mixture thoroughly and place where it will rise; the batter should rise and fall again before morning. In the morning sift into the batter one tsp. dry soda. Stir well and bake. If you have them every morning, save a little batter to raise them with in place of fresh yeast every time. *Mrs. H. S. Denny.*

CORN FRITTERS.

Cut the corn from four or five ears of corn, break an egg into it and add salt and pepper to suit the taste. Drop from a large spoon into a frying pan with butter in it. Fry on both sides to a rich brown.

Mrs. T. F. Colledge.

CORN FRITTERS.

Grate the corn. Stir in a small lump of butter, season with pepper and salt, and mix to the right consistency for cake batter, with fresh milk. Bake on a well greased griddle. *"Friendship Hill."*

CORN CAKES.

These cakes are not good except when made in the early fall from the first, fresh corn meal. Mix the corn meal to the proper consistency for cake batter with fresh milk. Add melted butter—a lump about the size of a walnut, season with salt and bake on well greased griddle. "*Friendship Hill.*"

RICE CAKES.

One c. cold boiled rice, (boiled in water) add enough cold water to make a batter, a pinch of salt, the whites of three eggs beaten stiff, and one tbsp. flour or entire wheat flour. A scant one-half tsp. baking powder to be mixed in just before cooking. Bake on soapstone griddle without any grease and serve with cinnamon and very little sugar. *Dr. Van Valzah.*

GERMAN PANCAKES.

Mix together two and one-quarter c. of flour and one tsp. of salt; separate the whites and yolks of six eggs, beat the yolks very light, add one qt. of milk, stir gradually into the flour and beat until smooth. Whip the whites to a stiff dry froth, cut them into the batter and beat lightly until well mixed. Into a medium sized frying-pan which has been heating over the the fire, drop one tsp. of lard or sweet dripping, turning the pan until well greased. When smoking hot pour in sufficient batter to cover the bottom of the pan and shake until light brown on the bottom. Turn and brown on the other side. Transfer to a hot plate and bake the remaining batter in the same way. Butter each cake as it is taken from the pan, piling them on each other; if desired they may also be spread with a little marmalade, jelly or powdered sugar.

RICE CAKES.

Put a pt. of boiled rice into a pt. of sweet milk to stand over night; in the morning add a pt. and a half flour,

ROLLS, MUFFINS, ETC.

one tsp. salt, one tbsp melted butter ; beat the mixture well, and add three well beaten eggs, and one pt. of milk, in which one tsp. Royal baking powder has been stirred. Cold oatmeal can be used same way.
Mrs. H. S. Denny.

GRAHAM GRIDDLE CAKES.

Mix together one c. of white and one c. Graham flour, one-half tsp. salt, beat two eggs, whites and yolks separately ; dissolve one tsp. soda in a little water, and stir into one pt. of sour milk ; add this to the dry mixture, and when well mixed, add the beaten eggs, and a tbsp. melted butter. *Mrs. H. S. Denny.*

FRITTERS.

Two eggs. When the yellows are well beaten, stir into them one pt. of cold milk, then stir in three c. of sifted flour, (if you like them thinner just half the quantity), add a pinch of salt, then stir in the well beaten whites, putting in last a heaping tsp. of baking powder.

Do not make them up too long before cooking. Have the lard boiling and drop in a spoonful of the batter at a time. *Mrs. H. B. Wilkins.*

WAFFLES.

Three eggs, one pt. milk, one qt. flour, small piece butter, one-half tsp. salt, one tsp. sugar, two tsp. baking powder add last thing. The best way to mix the waffles is in a pitcher, using a Dover egg beater.
" Cloud Capped."

ROLLS, MUFFINS, ETC.

RISEN WAFFLES.

Three eggs, one qt flour, one tbsp. lard, one-half c. rice boiled very soft and mashed, a little yeast. Let stand over night, adding the rice in the morning.

Mrs. J. B. Washington.

RICE WAFFLES.

One c. rice boiled soft and mashed, one tbsp. butter or lard melted, one pt. milk, four eggs well beaten, thicken with flour. *Mrs. J. B. Washington.*

SALLY LUNN.

Three eggs beaten separately, one qt. flour, one gill yeast, one tbsp. lard, a little salt, milk to make thick batter. *Mrs. J. B. Washington.*

GERMAN TOAST.

One egg, one-fourth tsp. salt, one c. milk, six or eight slices of stale bread. Beat the egg lightly, add salt and milk. Soak the bread in it until soft. Have a griddle hot and well buttered. Brown the bread well on one side, place a small piece of butter on the top of each slice, and turn and brown it on the other side. This toast is to be eaten hot, with butter, with cinnamon and sugar, or with a sauce.

MILK TOAST.

The bread is first dipped in milk with a little salt in it, and then toasted in a toaster by a bright fire quickly, and buttered. It ought to be eaten at once, without standing, as it is not as light after it gets cold. *Mrs. Plitt.*

EGGS AND CHEESE.

EGGS A LA MARTIN.

Have your dish hot. Put into a small saucepan a tsp. of butter. Let it melt, but be careful it does not brown; add a tsp. of flour, and then slowly, after the flour is well mingled, a c. of milk or cream. Add four tbsp. of grated cheese. Stir well, and, when heated, pour into your hot dish, and with great care, drop into the mixture four eggs. Put into the oven and, when the eggs are set, serve at once.

EGG PUFFS.

Add a dash of salt to the white of an egg, whip to a stiff froth. Place this in a deep saucer or c. and place in the centre the unbroken yolk. Set the dish in a pan of boiling water, cover and let cook two m. Serve in the same dish. Nice for an invalid.

BAKED EGGS.

Grease pie pan with butter, cover with rolled cracker crumbs and then break in eggs, season with salt and pepper, cover with cracker crumbs and bake.

Lizzie G. Williams.

EGGS AND CHEESE.

BAKED EGGS.

Cut hard boiled eggs in slices and arrange on a flat dish over which pour chicken gravy and brown in oven.

Emma Piper, Pro.

ORANGE OMELET.

The thinly grated rind of one orange, three tbsp juice, three tsp. powdered sugar, three eggs. Beat yolks of eggs until thick and creamy. Add the sugar, rind and juice and cut in whites of eggs, which have been beaten until stiff and dry. Place in French omelet pan, in which one tsp. of butter has been melted, and let cook until firm. Use very moderate heat, and be careful not to burn. Dry top of omelet in upper part of oven, fold and turn on to a heated platter. Dredge thickly with powdered sugar and score with a clean, red hot iron, in diagonal lines. Serve at once.

CHEESE.

"Rich American Cheese" is the best for all cooking purposes.

WELSH RAREBIT.

One-fourth lb. cheese (grated), one-fourth c. cream or milk, one-half or one tsp. mustard, one-half tsp. salt, cayenne, one egg, one tsp. butter. Dry toast. Put the cheese and milk or cream in a double boiler. Mix the mustard, salt and cayenne well and add the egg, thoroughly beaten. When the cheese is melted, stir in the mixture of dry ingredients and egg, then the butter and cook until it thickens. Stir constantly. Pour over the toast and serve immediately.

EGGS AND CHEESE. 39

CHEESE SOUFFLE.

Two tbsp butter, one and one-half tbsp. flour, one-half c. milk, one c. grated cheese, three eggs, one-half tsp. salt, cayenne and a pinch of soda. Put butter in the saucepan and when hot add the flour and stir until smooth; add the milk and seasoning. Cook two m. Remove to back of stove and add well beaten yolks and cheese. Set away to cool. When cold, add the whites of the eggs beaten to stiff froth. Turn into buttered bake dish and bake from twenty to twenty-five m. Serve the moment it comes from the oven. Bake in very moderate oven. The souffle should rise in fifteen m.

CHEESE PUDDING.

One pt. milk, two eggs, one pt. bread crumbs, one and one-half c. grated cheese, one-half tsp. salt, small pinch soda. Put milk into a well buttered bake dish, add the beaten eggs; then the crumbs, grated cheese, salt and soda, which have been mixed. Bake in very moderate oven until brown on top.

CHEESE PUFFS.

One-fourth lb. bread crumbs, one-fourth lb butter, two-thirds tsp. mustard, one-half tsp. salt, one-half lb. grated cheese, two gills milk, pinch cayenne, four eggs beaten separately. Boil the bread soft in the milk, add all the ingredients excepting the whites of the eggs. Beat thoroughly, then add the whites. Serve at once.

Miss J. McC. Taylor.

CHEESE FONDUE.

In a bowl put one c. of stale bread crumbs, add one c. of milk and let stand for twenty minutes. Then melt in the chafing-dish one tbsp. of butter and add the soaked bread crumbs. When hot stir in one c. of grated American cheese, one-half a tsp. of salt and a dash of cayenne. When the cheese is melted add two eggs well beaten; as soon as the mixture begins to thicken put out the light and serve on toasted crackers.

MEATS, ENTREES.

ROAST TURKEY.

Rub the turkey well with lard and then with pepper and salt. Make a dressing with bread crumbs, butter the size of an egg, lard half that size, a little pepper and salt and sweet marjoram to taste. Put the turkey in a pan with a little hot water and baste frequently while roasting. For small turkey roast one and one-half h. in quick oven. *Mrs. J. B. Washington.*

ROAST QUAIL.

Cut celery into small squares, about two tbsp. to each bird; one tbsp. chopped parsley to four birds. Butter the size of a hickory nut to each bird. Pepper and salt to taste. Stuff the birds, put bits of butter over them and a little sifted flour. Add a little water in the baking pan and baste frequently. Cook about twenty m. in a quick oven. *Mrs. J. B. Washington.*

ROAST CALF'S LIVER.

Have the butcher cut a pocket in the thick end of the liver, to hold the stuffing. Melt two tbsp. butter, to which add two c. fine bread crumbs, two hard boiled eggs chopped fine, two tsp. salt and one-half tsp. pepper.

MEATS, ENTREES.

Stuff the liver with this and after it has been tied or sewed together place it in the oven with one c. soup stock and a spoonful of currant jelly in the bottom of the pan. Baste *frequently* while roasting. Make brown gravy using the stock with which the liver has been basted and adding a little more currant jelly.

ROAST SPICED LIVER.

Take one calf's liver. Prick it in fifteen or twenty places with a sharp pointed knife In ten of the holes thus made place small bits of onion; then fill three holes with one clove each and in the remaining holes place bits of dried red or green pepper. Baste constantly with the following mixture: one c. water, one tbsp. butter and one tsp. flour. When cold slice thin and serve.

L W. Washington.

PATE OF LIVER.

Cut one lb of calf's liver, half lb. of fat salt pork and one onion into dice, season with a pinch of salt and fry four m. over a quick fire, shaking all the time Pound and rub through a wire sieve; while hot add two dozen truffles chipped fine and half a pt of good stock. Beat the mixture about ten m. and place in a mould. Let it stand on ice three or four hours. Turn and serve. This dish may be varied by cooking jelly in the mould before putting in the mixture. Also you can whip one-half pt. clear consomme or chicken broth which should be jellied with one-half pt. good stock, jellied till both are light and spongy; add this to a pt. of stiff whipped cream, cayenne pepper and a pinch of salt, and a small tin of pate' de foie gras. Stir together lightly and use around the mould as a garnish.

MEATS, ENTREES.

CHICKEN LIVERS.

Chop a small onion and fry it in butter without allowing it to color; put in the livers and some parsley and fry until they are done Take out the livers, add a little hot water or stock to the onions and parsley, thicken it with some flour; strain, season and pour over the livers.

CALF'S HEART STUFFED.

Merely wash off the blood, don't soak the heart. Stuff it with a veal force meat stuffing, or common stuffing used for turkeys; made of bread crumbs, onions, a little thyme, sage, egg, pepper and salt; and tie a buttered paper over the mouth of the heart to keep the stuffing in place. Put it in a small baking pan with a little hot water, pepper and salt, and bake nearly two h., basting frequently. When done, thicken the gravy with flour, strain, skim and season it, and pour it on a dish around the heart Garnish the dish with onions first boiled until nearly done, then seasoned with pepper, salt, and a little butter and browned in the oven. *Mrs Carroll Winchester.*

SCALLOPED CALF'S HEAD.

Cook the calf's head, tongue and heart together ; the brains separately. Cook all slowly with as little water as will cover them. When nearly done, take from the fire, and cut off all the meat from the bones. Cut up the other parts, and put into a baking dish in alternate layers. Pour in the liquid in which the meat was cooked. Season well with salt and pepper, and when almost done in the oven, pour on a generous glass of Madeira or sherry. Bread crumbs and butter are to be put between the layers, and finish with a layer of bread crumbs and butter.

MEATS, ENTREES.

CANAPÈS LORENZO.

Chop a medium sized shallot, fry lightly, without coloring, in two oz. of butter, add one tbsp. flour and wet with one pt. of cream, add one lb. of crab meat, salt and cayenne pepper, and leave on the fire until it just begins to bubble. Cut slices of bread one-fourth inch thick and trim round, square or oval. Toast only one side of bread, put your ingredients on the toasted side and cover them with a layer one-eighth of an inch thick with the following: one-fourth lb. of butter and one-half lb. grated parmesan cheese well mixed together, and seasoned with red and white pepper. Put your canapè in a buttered pan and color in the oven.

Mrs. Charles A. Painter.

CHOP À LA MAINTENON.

Put one tbsp. of butter in a frying-pan, when hot add one tbsp. of flour. Let the flour and butter cook for a few m., then add one c. of bread crumbs, one small onion chopped fine, enough cream to make a paste, and salt and pepper to taste, and set away to cool. Have six French chops broiled on one side and spread the mixture on the cooked side. Lay in a roasting pan and place in the oven to brown. Serve with rich sauce.

Mrs. Geo. A. Howe.

MUTTON CUTLETS À LA MAINTENON.

For six cutlets use four tbsp. of chopped mushrooms, one of chopped onion, one generous tbsp. of butter, one of flour, three of stock, one tsp. of minced parsley, one of salt, one-fifth of tsp. of pepper and three gills of Spanish sauce. Cook butter and onion together five m.;

MEATS, ENTREES.

then add mushrooms and seasoning and cook for five m. longer ; now add flour and stir well and then add stock and cook three m. longer. Let this mixture cool. Have cutlets from the ribs cut one inch and a half thick. Trim chops and with a sharp knife split them, without separating from the bone. Spread the cooked mixture inside, press together lightly and broil over a clear fire eight m. Arrange on a warm dish and pour the Spanish sauce around them. Serve very hot.

Mrs. H. S. Denny.

TO COOK VEAL CUTLETS.

Wash and wipe the cutlet; dip it in a beaten egg—let it soak well—then shake on it cracker dust, mace, salt and a little pepper. Fry it a nice brown, in lard; take it out and keep it hot. Strain the lard it was fried in, put it into a clean pan with a lump of butter, flour and one-half pt. milk and fine cut up parsley; stir it very smooth; put it into the dish under the cutlets (it should be creamy looking). *Mrs. Johnston.*

CORN BEEF.

OLD VIRGINIA RECIPE.

Get the best of beef—it must be fat. Salt the beef down on a table for twenty-four h. and then put into a tight barrel. Make a pickle of nine gal. water, nine lb. salt, three lb. brown sugar, one qt. molasses, three oz. saltpetre. Boil and skim the top off. When cold pour over the beef, which must be kept well under the brine. It will be fit for use in ten days.

Mrs. J. B. Washington.

MEATS, ENTREES.

WHITE PUDDINGS.

Thoroughly mix in the proportion of one qt. flour to one pt. suet, chopped *very fine*. Season in pepper and salt and stuff in sausage skins. Sausage stuffers can be gotten at any of the house-furnishing stores.

TO COOK SPRING CHICKENS.

If the chickens are very small cut them in half. If they are larger cut them in four or even six pieces. Place them in the oven, in a roasting pan, with a c. of water in the bottom of the pan and another pan over top of them. Beat butter and flour together *very light*, to about the consistency of thick cake batter and season with pepper and salt. When the chickens are almost done, take from the oven, drain off the stock, spread them over thickly with the batter and return them to a quick oven to brown. Make cream gravy of the stock, season with salt, pepper and chopped parsley, and serve with the chicken. *Mrs. Geo. A. Howe.*

FILLING FOR CHICKEN.

Take a quantity of dry bread crumbs, put into a pan with a good sized lump of butter; pepper and salt to taste and brown well. *Mrs. N. M. Marker.*

BOILED CHICKEN.

Stuff a chicken as for roasting, sprinkle over with plenty of salt, pepper and lemon juice. After tying legs and wings to side of chicken, dip a napkin into cold water and after wringing it well dredge thickly with flour. Pin the chicken up in a napkin, plunge into boiling water for fifteen minutes and then set back where it will simmer for two hours. Serve with egg sauce. This is

MEATS, ENTREES.

a good way to do chickens in winter. The water in which the chickens are boiled makes a good stock for cream of rice soup.

FRIZZLED BEEF.

Cut about one third of a lb. of dried beef into slices as thin as shavings. Beat together six eggs and a quarter of a c. of milk, season slightly with salt and pepper; melt two tbsp. of butter, when melted add beef and stir over hot fire until meat begins to curl, then draw back and add eggs and milk and stir until eggs begin to thicken.

HAMBURG STEAKS.

Two lb. of the round of beef chopped very fine; season with half a tsp. of pepper, two tsp. of salt, one fourth tsp. of celery seed, and one tsp. of onion juice. After shaping into thin cakes, place in boiler that has been buttered slightly, and broil over a clear fire eight m. Serve on a hot dish. *Mrs. H. S. Denny.*

DUTCH PUDDING.

Boil a piece of the neck of a beef until perfectly tender, and the bones come out easily. Take it up on a tray, let it cool, then pick it to pieces. Skim the grease off the liquor, and pour the latter into another vessel; after cleaning the kettle, return the meat and liquor; when it boils thicken with sifted meal until it is like mush; cook till well done, stirring constantly to prevent scorching. Season with salt, pepper and sage. Turn out into pans or crocks and when cold slice and fry brown like sausage. This is fine and very convenient for breakfast.

Mrs. D. Negley.

MEATS, ENTREES.

LIVER HASH.

Cut cold fried or stewed liver into small pieces; for one pt. of liver cook together a tbsp. of butter and a tsp. of flour until brown; add a scant c. of cold water and salt and pepper to taste. As soon as the gravy boils up put the liver into it and cook gently for twenty m. and then add one tsp. of lemon juice and one tsp. of Worcestershire sauce. Serve very hot. *Mrs. H. S. Denny.*

TURKEY HASH.

Cut a qt. of cold turkey into dice, season with salt and pepper. Put two tbsp. of butter into frying pan and when it is hot, not brown, add a tbsp. of flour; stir until the mixture is smooth and frothy and gradually add a pt. of cold milk; then let it boil up once and after seasoning add the seasoned turkey. Cook for eight m. Serve on buttered toast at once. *Mrs. H. S. Denny.*

BAKED HASH.

Two c. of cold meat hashed, one c. cold mashed potatoes, one stalk of celery and one small onion both minced fine; two tbsp. of butter, one-half c. of water and two tbsp. of bread crumbs. Mold and bake one-half h. Serve with tomato sauce which will be given on page with other sauces. *Mrs. H. S. Denny.*

HASH.

One c. of meat chopped fine, two c. hot mashed potatoes, one-third c. boiling water or more, one-half tbsp. beef fat, one tbsp. butter, salt and pepper and onion juice. Heat the beef drippings in a French omelet pan. Mix all the other ingredients, beating thoroughly, then spread smoothly in the pan. Cook over moderate heat

MEATS, ENTREES.

for about one-half an h. so that it will brown slowly and not burn. Do not stir. Fold like an omelet and turn on to serving dish, garnishing with parsley.

STEWED KIDNEY.

Soak a beef kidney in cold water one h.; then, with a sharp knife, cut it in small pieces. Reject all fat and gristle. While cutting the kidney, throw each piece into cold water. Wash well, and put into a saucepan with a pt. of cold water. Slice half a small onion, and add a bay leaf, a sprig of parsley, a half tsp. of celery seed, or a piece of celery, and one clove. Skim when it boils up, then cover and boil slowly three h. Turn into a dish. Next morning, make a sauce of one tbsp. of butter and flour, and heat thoroughly. Season with salt, pepper, Worcestershire sauce and lemon juice, and serve very hot.

SWEETBREADS.

Wipe the sweetbreads dry, and roll them in grated cracker, a little dry mustard, salt and pepper and fry them. Melt butter (do not use lard) with cream and parsley, and pour on the dish, putting the sweetbreads on top. *Mrs. Johnston.*

BAKED SWEETBREADS.

Let sweetbreads stand in cold water for half an h. and then parboil for ten m., season well with pepper and salt, roll in beaten white of egg, then in cracker crumbs, dot with small lumps of butter and bake in moderate oven about one-half h.; serve on toast.
Mrs. E. B. McColly.

MEATS, ENTREES.

RISSOLLES.

To one boiled chicken, chopped very fine, add two large sweetbreads, about half and half, also chopped fine. Put one-half pt. cream on the fire with four oz. of butter, and, when it boils, stir in *gradually* the chicken and sweetbreads, to which has been added two tbsp. of flour, two tsp. cold ham, chopped *as fine as possible*, and the *least suspicion* (say a tsp.) of garlic, chopped very fine, red pepper and salt to taste. These must be boiled in the cream, stirring all the time to keep from burning, until it falls easily from the spoon, which shows that it is sufficiently done, and then put it on a dish to cool.

Have ready some puff paste *rolled as thin as is possible*, which cut into round pieces about the size of a small plate. Place about a spoonful on *one-half* of this, turn over the other half, forming a "half moon."

Have ready the beaten yolks of some eggs, with a very little water in a flat dish, and another *plate* (or flat dish) with vermicelli broken into pieces about two inches long. Put the rissolie into the egg first, and then into the vermicelli, covering it completely, and then place it in the lard to fry. The lard must be boiling, not too hot, but sufficiently so not to allow the rissolle to lie a moment in it without cooking. When slightly brown they are done, and they do not take much more than two m. to cook.

Mrs. H. L. Johnston.

CHICKEN CROQUETTES.

Parboil and mash four sweetbreads, boil in one-half pt. cream, butter the size of an egg, small piece of onion, one blade celery, a little white pepper and a very little

MEATS, ENTREES.

nutmeg. Strain this from the cream and thicken with two tbsp. flour, then add the sweetbreads and cook for a few m. Stir enough chopped chicken or turkey into this, not to make it too stiff and set away to cool. Beat the yolk of one egg on a dish and add a little milk. Form your croquette, roll in crumbs, then in egg and again in crumbs. Set aside in a cool place. Boil a few at a time in a small vessel of hot lard. *Mrs. J. B. Washington.*

CROQUETTES.

Are made exactly like *Rissolles*, except an onion browned in three oz. butter, chopped fine, is used in place of the garlic and ham, and, if you like, parsley. They are made into croquette form and fried slightly brown.
Mrs. H. L. Johnston.

CROQUETTES.

For one and one-half doz. or more croquettes, chop up four boiled sweetbreads and one pair chickens very fine; add the brains of a calf and pt. or more of cream. Mix them up as light as batter, have the bread crumbs rolled out, put the batter in and form them into croquettes; fry them in fresh *boiling* lard. *Mrs. H. L. Johnston.*

CROQUETTES.—(Meat and Hominy.)

Put half a c. of milk into a frying pan, when heated to the boiling point stir in a c. of boiled hominy-grits, a c. of finely chopped meat, a tsp. of salt, an eighth of a tsp. of pepper and two tbsp. of butter. Stir well and when the mixture begins to boil add one well beaten egg. When cold shape and roll in egg and cracker meal. Fry in fat until brown. *Emma Piper, Pro.*

MEATS, ENTREES.

SWEET POTATO CROQUETTES.

One pt. of mashed potatoes, half a c. of hot milk, two generous tbsp. of butter, one tsp. of salt, two eggs. When the potatoes have been mashed smooth and light beat in the hot milk, salt and pepper, then one egg beaten light. Beat the second egg and use for breading the croquettes. Fry in fat until they turn a rich brown.

Mrs. H. S. Denny.

TO DRESS TERRAPIN.

Melt a lump of butter in the saucepan with the terrapin and stir in flour with pepper and salt to taste, add a c. of cream—more or less, as you choose. For three terrapins, one c. will be enough. For six terrapins you will need one pt. cream and more butter and flour.

Mrs. H. L. Johnston.

CHICKEN FOR LUNCH.

Stew one chicken in pt. of water in a double boiler and when tender lift the chicken out and pour one pt. of rich cream into the chicken broth. Thicken with a little flour and milk, and just before taking out stir in the yolks of two eggs. Strain the whole thing, salt and pepper the chicken before boiling and put a lump of butter in the water in which the chicken is boiled.

Miss J. McC. Taylor.

CHICKEN TERRAPIN.

Three pts. cold boiled chicken, three hard boiled eggs, three heaping tbsp. flour that has been browned in the oven, one-half pt. chicken stock, one pt. rich milk, salt, cayenne pepper, one-half tsp. mace, one c. butter, a wine glass of madeira. Cut the chicken fine, rub eggs through

MEATS, ENTREES.

a sieve. Melt the butter and add the flour, next the milk which has been scalded, and the stock. When this mixture has thickened add the minced chicken, egg and seasoning. Cook slowly for one-half an h., add the wine and serve on toast.

MOCK TERRAPIN.

Season and fry brown a calf's liver, then hash it fine and dust thickly with flour. Mix two tsp. mustard, a little cayenne pepper, three hard boiled eggs chopped fine, a piece of butter the size of an egg and a c. of water. Let it cook a little, add the chopped liver and simmer a few m. together and serve hot. A little wine improves it. *Miss Loulie Macgill.*

MARROW ON TOAST.

Boil a marrow bone. Remove the marrow, slice thin, and serve at once on fresh buttered toast, which has been slightly softened with hot water. Season with salt and red pepper. *L. W. Washington.*

DEVILED DRESSING.

Make one c. brown sauce to which add one tbsp. vinegar, one ssp. mustard, one ssp. black pepper and salt and red pepper to taste. This dressing can be used with ham, turkey, or roast beef. When turkey or beef are used the brown gravy may be used instead of the brown sauce. In deviling meat it should first be thoroughly heated on the broiler and then turned into the saucepan with the dressing where it can finish cooking. Turkey wings and legs or the breast cut thick is best. When beef is used it should be very rare and cut thick.
L. W. Washington.

MEATS, ENTREES.

FRIED FROGS' LEGS.

No. 1. Wash and boil ten m. in salted water; drain and when cool dip the legs separately into cracker dust, then into beaten egg, again into cracker dust and fry to a nice brown in a kettle of hot lard or butter. Send to the table hot, garnished with parsley or cress.

No. 2. Fry the skinned frog's legs in butter; cook some fresh mushrooms in the pan at the same time if convenient. Place on a hot dish with the mushrooms and pour over them a Poulette sauce. *Miss Hargnett.*

JELLIED CHICKEN.

After boiling a chicken in as little water as possible, until the meat falls from the bones, shred the meat into small pieces and season with pepper and salt. Put in the bottom of the mould slices of hard boiled egg and lemon, then a layer of chicken. Fill the mould to the top with alternate layers of chicken and egg. Boil down the stock until there is about a c. left. Season it well and pour it over the chicken. It will sink through the meat forming a jelly around it. If there is any danger of it not being stiff enough, a little gelatin may be soaked and added to the stock.

Mrs. Carroll Winchester.

MINCED CHICKEN WITH JELLY.

Boil a chicken in as little water as possible, with mace, salt, pepper, onion and celery. When done, take the meat from the bones, put the bones in the chicken water, and let it cook to a jelly. Cut the meat and liver as fine as possible. Mince and pound in the mortar till quite soft. Season with half a small boiled onion, chopped fine, two wine-glasses of cream, pepper, salt, the yolk of a

MEATS, ENTREES. 59

hard boiled egg, one dessert spoon of "Reading" sauce, one of mushroom sauce or any other you prefer, a little nutmeg and one-fourth lb. of butter. Strain the stock, put part of it in a mould. When stiff, press the meat on top of jelly, leaving a little space round it; then pour the rest of stock round it. "*I* put my chicken in a bowl and turn it out and put jelly round it, and I put calves' feet (or Cox's gelatin) in with the chicken bones to help stiffen it, especially in warm weather. Of course, you must take all the grease off the jelly, and, if cloudy, clear with white of an egg." *Mrs. Neil.*

JELLIED CHICKEN.

Boil a chicken in enough water to make three pt. of stock when done. Soak one box of gelatin in one-half c. of cold water. Clear the stock with white of egg, pour over the gelatin while hot and season with salt, red and black pepper, the juice of two lemons and one pt. cooking sherry. Line the mould with slices of hard boiled egg and lemon then put in the chicken, shredded in small pieces and pour in as much jelly as the mould will hold. Pour the rest of the jelly into a bowl and place the moulds on or near the ice. When ready to serve, turn out the mould with the chicken in it and trim the dish with spoonsful of the clear jelly.

JELLIED VEAL.

Use a knuckle of veal weighing about four lbs, three hard boiled eggs, juice of one lemon, two tbsp. of minced onion, one of parsley, a bit of mace, a piece of stick cinnamon, half a dozen cloves, two sprigs of thyme, a level tsp. of pepper, two tbsp. of salt and three pt. of water. Break veal in several pieces and put into a kettle with the water. Tie up all the seasoning, except the salt, pepper and lemon, in a muslin bag and put them in the kettle with the veal. When the contents boil, skim carefully and cook slowly four hours. Then take up the meat, free it from the bones and cut into small pieces. Put the meat into a clean stew pan and strain over it the water in which it was boiled; add lemon juice, pepper and salt and simmer for half an h. Slice the eggs and arrange in a mould, then a layer of veal and then egg until all has been used. Set in a cold place three or four h. At serving time turn on a flat dish and garnish with parsley. *Mrs. H. S. Denny.*

VEAL LOAF.

Five lbs. veal cut from leg—one c. cracker crumbs powdered fine, one and one-half c. stock, three eggs, three-fourths lb. fat salt pork, one-fourth c. dried bread crumbs, one tbsp. chopped onion, one scant tsp. thyme, one-half tsp. sweet marjoram, one-half tsp. summer savory, three generous tsp. salt, one of white pepper, two tbsp. butter. Chop veal and pork fine and add cracker crumbs, seasoning, two of the eggs well beaten, one c. stock; mix well with hands. Butter a flat-cake pan; form mixture into a loaf four inches high and five wide and place in pan. Beat third egg well and spread on loaf with brush; sprinkle loaf with fine bread crumbs. Put in rather hot oven and bake three hours, basting frequently, with one-half c. stock and two tbsp. melted butter. A little celery seed or celery sauce is an addition to the mixture.

MEATS, ENTREES.

PORK.

WM. BAKER DORSEY'S RECEIPT FOR CURING HAMS.

One tsp. of best saltpetre, one tbsp. of brown sugar, to be rubbed on the fleshy side of each ham, fine salt and ground alum salt mixed half and half to be rubbed on leaving salt on the ham about as thick as would track a rabbit; pack away into a hogshead or trough that will hold the brine. Let them remain six (6) weeks, then hang up hock downwards, not touching, and smoke with green hickory wood until about the 10th of March or before the fly appears. Then take each ham and pack them away in a tight box with a cover to keep out rats and mice. Put sticks between them so that they do not touch, then pour dry hickory ashes over, so as to cover them entirely.

After the hams have been thus put away, say three weeks, examine them in warm sultry weather. They will sweat and form a mould over them. Put them out in the sun for a few hours, to give them a good airing; sun must not be too hot; then re-pack as before, pouring the same ashes over them. Do this as often as necessary. This is for *hams* of hogs weighing 150 lbs.; all else is to be determined by good judgment.

Mrs. H. L. Johnston.

PORK.

CURING HAMS.

For 1,000 Lbs.

Three pks. salt, three and one-half lbs. saltpetre, two qts. hickory ashes, two qts. molasses, two c. red pepper, mixed well together. Rub each piece of meat well with the above ingredients and pack down in a tub. Keep in salt for six weeks, then hang up and smoke for six weeks with hickory wood.

For 200 Lbs.

Four and three-fourths qts. salt, three-fourths lb. saltpetre, one-half c. red pepper, one pt. ashes, one pt. molasses.

For 150 Lbs.

Three qts. salt, one-half lb. saltpetre, one pt. sugar, two large spoonfuls red pepper, one pt. ashes.

An old Virginia receipt. *Mrs. J. B. Washington.*

TO CURE HAMS.

This is the way Mrs. Henry Clay made the celebrated Ashland hams: For every ten hams of moderate size she took three and a half lbs. of fine salt, one lb. of saltpetre, and two lbs. brown sugar, and after mixing thoroughly together, rubbed the hams therewith on both sides. They were then packed in a tight box and put in a cool outhouse for about three weeks, then taken out and put in a pickling tub or hogshead, and covered with brine strong enough to float an egg. After three weeks they were taken out, thoroughly rubbed with fresh salt, and hung up in a well ventilated house for a few days to dry, then hung in the smoke house and smoked with green hickory or walnut wood

PORK.

until the color of bright mahogany, when each ham was sewed up in canvas, the bag whitewashed and hung up to dry.

RECEIPT FOR CURING BACON.

Hogs weighing from one hundred and thirty to one hundred and fifty lbs. are regarded as the most suitable size. The pork should be fat and nicely dressed. After the pork has lost the animal heat and is entirely cool throughout, cut it out, rounding the ham and cutting off the feet below the hock. To each ham, well rubbed on, put one tsp. saltpetre (or more if the ham is large) well rubbed on both sides and then salt well with equal parts of fine and ground alum salt, and pack the pieces as close as possible on a platform, the skin side down. It should remain thus five or six weeks and then taken up, strings securely inserted in the fat end through the skin, all the salt well brushed off and a paste of equal parts of common molasses and black pepper applied to the flesh side, and over this as well as the other, a heavy coat of strong hickory ashes and then hung up to be smoked with hickory or red oak wood over a moderate fire for about eight or ten weeks when it should be taken down before warm weather, carefully examined but not scraped and put in bags fitting tolerably close, and again hung up to remain until wanted. The bags must be sewed up closely and the meat however kept dark. They will be good in June, but much better in August or September. *Newman.*

From Mrs. R. C. Johnson.

PORK.

CHEESE SOUSE.

Take the head and jowl and boil them with salt, pepper and a little onion until the meat is tender, then cut it into thin slices. Skin and strain the liquor and season with allspice, cloves and pounded thyme and a little red pepper. Return the meat to the pot in which the liquor is, and boil down to a thick jelly, then put it into a mould. *Mrs. George E. H. Brandon.*

TO MAKE SOUSE CHEESE.

The feet and heads must be thoroughly cleansed and placed in a weak brine for 24 hs., drain out of this and put them on in cold water and in separate vessels, adding a little salt and boil gently until thoroughly done. The meat must leave the bone. Then in the proportion of one head to 12 feet, as soon as cold enough to bear the hands in it, pick to pieces and mash well, discarding every bone, and adding a small quantity of the liquor in which the feet have been boiled. Season with pepper, salt and a little vinegar, place it in moulds, put a plate or dish on them with weight and it will be ready to turn out in 24 hs. It must not freeze or it will fall to pieces. Prepare a weak brine, let it get perfectly cold, add vinegar to it until you can taste it, strain it and place in a tub or keg in which you can keep the souse immersed. The vinegar should be light or it will darken the souse which should be perfectly white. Some persons in cleaning the feet singe the hair off. This discolors them and imparts a taste. They should be cleansed by repeated scraping and scalding. Should you wish to souse the feet alone prepare in the same way and only boil until the skin can be pierced with a straw. They are kept in the same brine with the cheese. *Newman.*

PORK.

PUDDING.

One jowl, two tongues, four hearts, four livers, to be boiled until very tender and run through a sausage grinder. Then add one small onion, grated, salt and pepper to taste and mix with sufficient water, in which the heads and feet were boiled, to make quite soft, but not thin. Stuff in skins and dip (for a min) into the boiling water in which the livers, etc., were boiled. An old Virginia receipt. *Mrs. J. B. Washington.*

ROAST PIG.

Take a pig of about eight or ten lbs., clean well, leaving on the head and feet. Make a stuffing of bread, two eggs, one tbsp. of butter, sugar, thyme, onion chopped and pepper and salt, Stale bread is best. Stiffen with water and put in a frying-pan with a tbsp. of lard to brown, mixing in the eggs, butter and seasoning. When brown stuff the pig and sew up the opening. Truss with the front legs bent backward and the back legs forward. Brush the pig with butter or salad oil. Baste frequently. Cook until thoroughly done and make the gravy, (after removing the pig), by adding a little water thickened with flour, and the liver and heart of the pig (which have been cooked in the pan with it), chopped fine and mixed in. Serve in a gravy dish.

TO BOIL AND BAKE A HAM.

The ham should be soaked in cold water for twenty-four h. Then put on the fire and simmer slowly for seven or eight h. Take from the fire and remove the skin. Stuff the ham all over closely with whole cloves and place in a large pan.

Boil one qt. vinegar or cider with one and one-half pts. brown sugar, and pour over the ham. Place in a very moderate oven and baste every few m. while it is baking. It should bake for at least three or four h. One pt. sugar and one pt. vinegar is often enough.

"*Friendship Hill.*"

HAM PATTIES.

One pt. of ham, which has previously been cooked, mix with two-thirds pt. bread crumbs, which have been moistened with milk. Place this mixture in small china cups or skillets which have been buttered, break an egg over each one, sprinkle the tops thickly with bread crumbs. Add a little pepper and salt and small pieces of butter and bake in quick oven till browned over. A nice breakfast dish.

PORK.

VEGETABLES.

TO BOIL RICE.

Wash it well in cold water. Throw it into plenty of boiling water and boil it say twenty m. Then drain it through a colander, and set the colander on a saucepan or something to keep it hot on the back of the stove When used as a dessert cook it in the same way, and when drained spread it on a dish to cool. When cold, add rich milk, wine or brandy, sugar and nutmeg. To be served very cold. It is very nice with stewed chicken and curry. *Miss Hettie Parker.*

RICE.

One tea c. of rice, two qts of water, boil forty-five m. with a little salt and do not stir. After boiling turn into a colander and place under cold spigot and rinse thoroughly. Then set colander into a moderate oven for three quarters of an h. At the end of that time it will be white and dry and each grain separate.
Mrs. Geo. C. Burgwin.

VEGETABLES.

FRIJOLES.
National Dish of Mexico.

Soak two qts. of beans over night, then boil four h. with a small quantity of soda. Cut up some onions very fine and fry them a light brown; add to them a ladle of the beans, stir and mash with a wooden spoon. Add more, until all are perfectly smooth. Add salt and lard, enough lard to keep the beans all the time from burning or sticking to the pan. In another pan brown two heaping tbsp. flour; add this with two tbsp. molasses to the beans. Put them away in a jar and every time they are used beat up again with lard, and serve with fried bananas over the top. *Mrs. Jere S. Black.*

OKRA.

Take a pt. of pods and after removing the stems put them on to boil. If the pods are young boil them thoroughly for about an h. Prepare in the meantime a half pt. of any kind of stock and add a small onion with three or four cloves stuck in it, also a small tomato; stir thoroughly and when done pass it through a strainer, add pepper and salt, also a very small quantity of rum, only enough to make the sauce the consistency of rich gravy. Strain the water from the okra, then place the okra in a dish and serve with the sauce poured over it. The pods should be boiled until very soft.

Mrs. J. H Shoenberger.

LYONNAISE POTATOES.

Half a lb. of cold boiled potatoes, two tbsp. of minced onion, a heaping tsp. of minced parsley, butter the size of an egg. When the butter is hot, throw in the onion

VEGETABLES.

and fry to a light brown; then add potatoes. Turn until they are thoroughly heated and brown; then add parsley and seasoning of salt and pepper. *Mrs. H. S. Denny.*

POTATOES AU GRATIN.

Butter a large platter and spread upon it a qt. of cold potatoes cut into small cubs; dredge with salt and pepper and sprinkle a tsp. of fine chopped parsley over the dish; cover with a pt. of cream sauce and place in the oven for ten or twelve m. In that time the potatoes should become slightly browned.

SAUCE.—Melt two tbsp. of butter, when melted add one tbsp. of flour. Stir until smooth and frothy, then draw back to a cooler part of the stove and gradually add a pt. of milk. Season with salt and pepper and boil for a m. *Mrs. H. S. Denny.*

STEWED POTATOES.

Cut cold boiled potatoes into *small* dice. Potatoes which have been on ice at least six h. are the best for this purpose. Put a c. of cream and butter the size of a walnut in the stewpan, and when thoroughly heated add the potatoes. The potatoes should only remain on the stove long enough to thoroughly heat through and to slightly thicken the cream. Season with pepper, salt, and chopped parsley and serve at once.

"Friendship Hill."

STUFFED POTATOES.

Select and wash fine, large, old potatoes, bake until mealy, when cold cut in half, remove all the inside of the potato, taking care not to break the skin. To each potato add one tbsp. milk, one tsp. cream or butter; beat

VEGETABLES.

until very light, season with salt and pepper to taste and put on the stove in sauce pan, allowing it to remain until it just comes to a boil. Fill the potato skins with this mixture, cover over with grated cheese and put in hot oven to brown. *L. W. Washington.*

FRIED APPLES.

The apples must be firm and juicy Cut them in slices over quarter of an inch thick. Melt a heaping tbsp. of butter in the skillet and put in the apples, only as many as the skillet can conveniently hold; never crowding them When the apples have become well browned sprinkle them thoroughly with about a c. and a half of pulvarized sugar. When the sugar has become hot sprinkle it with one-half c. of water to melt it. Leave on the stove a few minutes longer until the sugar has formed a thick clear syrup. For a family of more than four, two skillets must be used. *Mrs. Geo. A. Castleman.*

SUMMER SQUASH.

Boil until tender. Mash through a colander and boil again until you can drain off all the water. Then mix with cream, butter, pepper and salt.
Mrs Geo. A. Castleman.

MUSHROOMS.

To give mushrooms a delicious flavor, take a small onion in which eight or ten whole cloves have been stuck, and stew it in the pan with the mushrooms.
Mrs. Geo. A. Castleman.

VEGETABLES.

GLAZED SWEET POTATOES.

Cut cold sweet potatoes in slices about an inch thick and season well with salt and pepper. For a qt. of potatoes, melt half a c. of butter and add two tbsp. of sugar to it; dip the slices in this liquid and lay them in a large pan. Cook twelve m. in a very hot oven. They should be a rich, glossy brown. *Mrs, H. S. Denny.*

MACARONI.

Twelve sticks macaroni, one and one-half c. thin white sauce, one-half c. stale bread crumbs, with one tbsp. butter and one c. grated cheese.

Break the macaroni in two in. pieces. Cook in boiling salted water about twenty m. (or until soft.) Pour into a colander and run cold water through it. Place in a buttered cooking dish, and add the sauce with half the cheese in it. Put the crumbs into the melted butter, add the remaining cheese to them and spread over the top. Replace in oven until it has become brown.

It will be found a great improvement to scald an onion stuffed with whole cloves in the milk for the white sauce.

CORN PUDDING.

One doz. and a half ears of corn, grated, a c. of cream, salt, pepper and a lump of butter size of a large egg. Bake three-quarters of an h., or until brown on top. (Emily Baker). *Mrs. Hopkins*

CORN PUDDING.

Nine large or twelve small ears of corn, one qt. rich milk. Scrape the corn, add the milk, salt and pepper and pieces of butter on top. The pudding should be baked one h. in a slow oven. As the corn gets older you will have to use your judgment about how much milk to add

"*Friendship Hill.*"

SCALLOPED CORNLET.

One can cornlet, two-thirds c. milk, two c. bread crumbs, two or three tbsp. butter, two and a half tsp. salt, one fourth tsp. pepper.

Mix the cornlet and milk, season with salt and pepper, and put into a buttered baking dish. Cut one tbsp. butter in small pieces and place it in the dish. The remaining butter is to be melted and the crumbs added to it for the top. Brown in a hot oven twenty or thirty m Cooked onion or cabbage which has been chopped may be used in the same way.

BROILED TOMATOES.

After paring and slicing the tomatoes, add seasoning of salt and pepper, dip the slices in beaten egg and cracker meal. Broil over clear coals for about eight m. Place on a hot dish with a bit of butter in the center of each slice. *Mrs. H. S. Denny.*

ESCALOPED CAULIFLOWER.

Put a good sized cauliflower into a kettle containing two qts. of boiling water, and after adding a tbsp. of salt, cook slowly for half an h.; then remove the cauliflower from the water and drain; place in an escalop-dish and sprinkle with grated cheese, then pour over a cream sauce and bake about twenty m.

To make the sauce: Put two tbsp. of butter in a saucepan; when melted add a tbsp. of flour; stir until

VEGETABLES. 81

the sauce is smooth and frothy, then gradually add a pt. of cold milk. Season with salt and let boil up once.

Mrs. H. S. Denny.

STUFFED EGG PLANT.

To one good sized egg plant use one pt. of grated bread crumbs, an egg, two tbsp. of butter, one tsp. of salt, a quarter of a tsp. of pepper, half a tsp. of chopped onion, and the same quantity of chopped parsley; boil the egg plant ten m., then take from the fire, and as soon as it has become partially cooled, cut in two pieces, cutting lengthwise; then scoop out the inside, being careful not to break the skin; cook the butter, onion and parsley in a frying pan three m.; then add the pulp of the egg plant, (which has been hashed fine) and the seasoning, and cook ten m. longer, stirring frequently; then add the well beaten egg and remove from the fire; put the two shells of the egg plant in a baking pan, fill with the cooked mixture, sprinkle the bread crumbs over them and bake in a hot oven for twenty m. or until well browned. Send to the table very hot. *Mrs. H. S. Denny.*

CELERY AU JUS.

Wash the celery and cut in pieces one inch long; cover with boiling stock, season with salt and boil thirty m. Put one tbsp. of butter into a pan and stir until brown, add to it one tbsp. of flour and mix until smooth. Drain the celery, then add one-half pt. of the liquor in which it was boiled to the butter and flour; stir until it boils, then add seasoning to taste. Put the celery into a heated dish, pour the sauce over it and serve at once.

Mrs. H. S. Denny.

VEGETABLES.

ASPARAGUS WITH EGGS.

Boil a bunch of asparagus twenty m., cut off the tender tips and lay them in a deep pie plate; butter, salt and pepper well. Beat four eggs, yolks and whites separately to a stiff froth; add two tbsp. of milk or cream, a tbsp. of melted butter, pepper and salt. Pour over the asparagus and bake in the oven until the eggs are set.

Hattie Keltz.

COLD SLAW.

Sift a tsp. of flour into one-half a teacup of milk or cream. Stir until perfectly smooth. Beat the yolks of three eggs. Have on the fire one-half a tumblerful of vinegar, with a piece of butter the size of an egg. When it is just coming to a boil, strain flour and milk into it, stirring hard a few m. Pour it over cabbage, and stand it in a cold place. *Mrs. H. L. Johnston.*

COLD SLAW.

Cut the cabbage and put it into the dish you send on table. Put into a saucepan the yolks of two eggs, one-fourth lb. of butter, two or three tbsp. of vinegar, according to the strength, (we never made ours very sour), a large pinch of salt and some pepper. If you have a great deal of cabbage, add one tbsp. of rich cream. Stir this mixture all the time it is on the fire, and just *before* coming to a boil throw it over the cabbage and mix it thoroughly; then sift white pepper on the top and set it by. It should be made several h. before it is used.

Mrs. Plitt.

VEGETABLES.

VEGETABLES.

SALADS, SALAD DRESSINGS AND SANDWICHES.

TOMATO JELLY.

Half a can or two c. tomatoes, three cloves, one bay leaf, one slice onion, one-half tsp. thyme, one tsp. salt, one tsp. sugar, one quarter tsp. pepper, one-half oz. gelatin soaked in one-half c. water. Boil together the tomatoes, spices and onion until the tomato is soft, then add the soaked gelatin and stir until the gelatin is dissolved, then strain and pour it into a border or ring shaped mould to set. Serve with the centre of the jelly ring filled with celery cut into pieces and mixed with mayonnaise dressing, form outside the ring a wreath of lettuce, or mould the tomato jelly in a solid piece and surround in with celery and lettuce.

TOMATOES STUFFED WITH SWEETBREADS

Select the desired number of round, firm tomatoes; remove the skins, cut a thin slice from the stem end and scoop out the inside; parboil a pair of sweetbreads in salted water for twenty m., plunge into cold water, and remove all skins and sinews; chop fine, add chopped celery, salt and pepper to taste; fill the tomatoes; set on the ice to become cold. Serve on a lettuce leaf with mayonnaise dressing. *Mrs. William A. Peterson.*

SALADS, ETC.

SALAD DRESSING, WHICH WILL KEEP A LONG TIME.

One pt. vinegar, (if not too strong), one pt. water, one level tbsp. mustard, one tbsp. celery seed, one tbsp. butter, one tbsp. salt, yolks ten eggs, two tbsp. sugar. Let your vinegar and water come to the boil and stir them into your eggs; beat well and add butter, sugar, salt, mustard and celery seed.

This sauce can be put in a patent fruit jar and is very nice for potato salad. Add one-half a cucumber cut fine to your potato. *Mrs. Charles A. Painter.*

FRENCH DRESSING.

Mix in the proportion of one tbsp. of vinegar to three of olive oil and one ssp. of both pepper and salt and a little chopped onion or chives. This dressing *must* be beaten thoroughly in a *hot c.* A little tobasco sauce will sometimes be found an addition.

FRENCH DRESSING.

Four tbsp. oil, one tbsp. vinegar, two ssp. black pepper, two ssp. salt, red pepper to taste and a small clove of garlic. Have your salad prepared and placed in the salad bowl. Mix your dry ingredients in the salad spoon over a small bowl, in which you have placed a piece of ice about the size of a hickory nut. Pour the vinegar into the salad spoon and after the dry ingredients are dissolved, add the oil gradually. When thoroughly mixed pour over the salad.

L. W. Washington.

MAYONNAISE DRESSING.

For one pt. of dressing, use three gills of oil, yolks of two raw eggs, one tsp. of dry mustard, half a tsp. of

SALADS, ETC.

salt, two tbsp. of lemon juice, two of vinegar, one-tenth of a tsp. of cayenne and four tbsp. of thick sweet cream. In order to have this a success have all the materials very cold. Put yolks of eggs and the dry ingredients into a bowl and beat until thoroughly blended, then add oil, a few drops at a time, beating all the time. Use alternately the oil and lemon juice and vinegar. When all has been used, add whipped cream.

Mrs. H. S. Denny.

MAYONNAISE DRESSING.

The yolks of two hard boiled and one raw egg, mixed thoroughly together with one and one-half tsp. salt. Beat in very slowly (drop by drop) from one-third to one-half a bottle of olive oil. The secret of thickening the dressing is in mixing the eggs and salt *thoroughly* at first, and in beating in the oil *gradually.* Season to taste with a little cayenne pepper, mustard, onion, Taragon vinegar and cider vinegar. The vinegar should be mixed in alternately with the oil. In doing this you will prevent the dressing from becoming too thin. *Jane.*

TARTAR SAUCE.

Rub (beat) the yolk of a *cold* hard boiled egg through a hair sieve into a basin, to which add the yolks of two *raw* eggs with a little salt and pepper; mix all together with a wooden spoon; have a pt. of good salad oil in a bottle; hold it with the left hand over the basin, dropping it in very gradually, and with the right continue stirring it round until it becomes rather thick, then moisten it with a little Taragon or common vinegar still keeping it stirred, then more oil, and so on until you have used all the oil, keeping the sauce rather thick;

then add a tbsp. of finely chopped gherkins (small pickled cucumbers), half a tbsp. of chopped capers, half a tbsp. of chopped shallot (small onions or garlic) and the same of chopped parsley, two tbsp. of French mustard, a little cayenne pepper, (sugar), and more salt, if required; it is then ready for use. This sauce requires to be rather highly seasoned. Common vinegar may be used. Half this quantity for a small family.

Philadelphia Club Receipt.

From Mrs. Tucker Carroll and Mrs. Neil.

EGG SANDWICHES.

Boil hard six eggs, chop fine and mix into a paste with thick and highly seasoned mayonnaise, spread between slices of thin white bread and butter. *Jane.*

MEAT SANDWICHES.

Game, turkey or chicken chopped fine and made into a paste with highly seasoned mayonnaise is very nice for sandwiches. *Jane.*

LEMON SANDWICHES.

Take a c. of butter and a tsp. of mustard. Make into a paste by adding a little hot water; add a pinch of cayenne pepper. Rub together with the yolk of one egg and two tbsp. of lemon juice. Some persons prefer a tsp. of curry in place of mustard. Rub the mixture together until it forms a smooth paste, and add more salt, if desired. Slice thinly and evenly a loaf of good wheat-bread, and another of Boston brown-bread, each at least twenty-four h. old, and spread the slices with the preparation given above. Having spread the mixture evenly and thinly on the bread, make the sandwiches of one

SALADS, ETC.

slice of white bread and one of brown. They may all be made of white bread, if preferred. Trim the edges evenly, and cut them diagonally. If the slices are large, cut them twice across, and pile the angular bits upon a plate or basket. *C. T.*

OLIVE SANDWICHES.

Chop fine one bottle of Pim-oloes (olives) and mix with some very thick and highly seasoned mayonnaise dressing. Spread the mixture between slices of thin white bread and butter.

DESSERTS.

VANILLA ICE CREAM.

One qt. of cream, one-half pound sugar, two tbsp. of vanilla, or one vanilla bean. Put the sugar, half the cream and the bean, split in halves, on to boil in a farina boiler; stir constantly for ten m. Take from the fire, take out the bean, and with a blunt knife scrape out the seeds and the soft part from the bean being careful not to waste one drop. Mix the seeds thoroughly with the cream and stand away to cool. When cold add the remaining cream and freeze. This will serve six people.

Mrs. Geo. C. Burgwin.

FILLING FOR RICH ICE CREAM.
For One Quart Cream.

Put into a saucepan on the fire one c. of granulated sugar and one-quarter c. of boiling water. Stir until the sugar is dissolved, then let it cook slowly for five m., making a sugar syrup. Beat the yolks of three eggs until light. Pour into them slowly, stirring all the time, the sugar syrup. Place them on the fire and stir all the time until the mixture is thick enough to float the spoon and has the consistency of thick cream. Remove it from the fire and beat until cold. This mixture can be used with any kind of ice cream to make it richer.

Mrs. George A. Howe.

CAFÉ PARFAIT.

Into a saucepan put the yolks of five eggs, four tbsp. of powdered sugar, and one-third c. of very strong black coffee.

Beat till light; then stir over hot fire till mixture is thick enough to mask spoon. Take from the fire and beat till cold and thick. Cut into it one pt. of thick cream whipped to a froth. Turn into a mould and pack in ice and salt for three h. *Mrs. Chas. A. Painter.*

MACAROON ICE CREAM.

One qt. cream, one-fourth c. finely rolled macaroons, one c. sugar, one gill sherry, one tsp. vanilla. Mix cream and sugar together, then the sherry and vanilla, and last of all the macaroons. Stir well and freeze as you would ice cream. *Mrs. E. M. Ferguson.*

FROZEN PEACHES

One pt. sugar, one of boiling water and two qts. ripe peaches, pared and sliced. Put water, sugar and half doz. cracked peach stones in a pan and boil fifteen m. Put the peaches through a sieve and strain hot syrup over them. Mix and when cold freeze.

Mrs. H. S. Denny.

FROZEN STRAWBERRIES.

One qt. strawberries, juice of two lemons, one lb. sugar, one qt. water. Add sugar and lemon juice to berries and stand aside one h. Mash the berries, add the

DESSERTS.

water, stir until sugar is thoroughly dissolved and freeze slowly. Red raspberries are very nice the same way.

Josephine Frank.

ORANGE WATER ICE.

Boil together one qt. water and three-fourths lb. of sugar for ten or twelve m., then take from fire and let it cool. Squeeze the juice from twelve oranges and three lemons, strain, rub a lump of loaf sugar in the rind of an orange and add to the mixture, pour in sugar and water, and freeze.

IMPERIAL PUDDING.

One-half c. rice, one pt. milk, one c. sugar, four tbsp. wine, one-half tsp. salt, two qts. and one pt. whipped cream, one-half box gelatin soaked for two h. in one-half c. cold water.

Wash the rice and put it on to boil in one qt. cold water, when it begins to boil pour off all the water. Add the pt. of milk and put into the double boiler and after an h. cooking add the gelatin, sugar, salt and wine. Place in a basin of ice water and stir until cold, then add whipped cream, stirring well. Pour into moulds and set away to harden.

The rind and juice of two oranges may be substituted for the wine. Cook the grated rind with the juice and milk. Add the juice to the cooked mixture.

ICED RICE PUDDING WITH A COMPOTE OF ORANGES.

One-half c. of rice, one qt. of cream, yolks of six eggs, one pt. of milk, two c. of sugar, one tbsp. of vanilla. Rub the rice well in a clean towel, put it on to boil in one pt. of cold water ; boil a half h. ; drain, cover with the milk and boil a half h. longer. While this is boiling, whip the qt. of cream. After you have whipped all you can, add the remainder, and what has drained from the other, to the rice and milk. Stand the whipped cream in a cold place until wanted. Now press the rice through a wire sieve, and return it to the farina boiler in which it was boiled. Beat the yolks and sugar together until light, then pour over the boiling rice; stir well. Return again to the fire, and cook two m. or until it begins to thicken. Take from the fire, add the vanilla, and turn out to cool ; when cool, put into the freezer and freeze. When frozen stir in the whipped cream, remove the dasher and smooth down and let stand for two h., packed in salt and ice.

For the Compote.

One doz. sweet oranges, juice of a quarter of a lemon, one lb. of sugar, one gill of water. Put the sugar and water on to boil ; boil ten m.; skim and add the lemon juice. Pare and slice the oranges, and put a few pieces at a time in the hot syrup, and lay them out singly on a flat dish. Pour over them the remaining syrup, and stand on the ice to cool. Heap the oranges on top and aroµnd the base of the pudding, and pour the syrup over them. Serve immediately.

The receipt for the compote we do not use, but prepare the orange as we would to serve them alone, and use the juice instead of the syrup. *Miss E. K. Holmes.*

PLUM PUDDING.

One lb. stoned raisins, one lb. washed currants, one-half lb. citron cut in strips, one lb. suet, eight eggs, one-half lb. grated (baker's) bread, one pt. of new milk, one nut-

DESSERTS.

meg, a wineglass of French brandy, four tbsp. flour; beat the eggs very light, add a lb. of nice brown sugar, and then the other ingredients by spoonful. When well mixed and having had the pudding bag or cloth well washed in boiling water and well floured, tie the pudding tight with a strong string, allowing some space for it to swell in boiling. When the pot is boiling up, put the pudding in, dipping it in three or four times before leaving in the pot. This pudding is a large one and requires five h. to cook properly. When dished, pour a rich sauce over it, or bring it in with brandy around it on fire.

Mrs. Nicholson.

PLUM PUDDING.

Take the crumbs of a small loaf of bread; rub it very fine, add fourteen eggs well beaten, one wineglass of brandy, one nutmeg, one tsp. ground cloves, one tsp. mace, two lb. suet chopped fine. Mix them all together well. Rub together seven tbsp. white sugar and one-fourth lb. melted butter. Add this with one and a half lb. currants, and one lb. raisins (seeded). The fruit should be well floured before adding. Add one tea c. flour; flour the bag well, put pudding in, tie tight and boil for three h. *Mrs. H. P. Allen.*

FIG PUDDING.

Six oz. suet, chopped fine, one-half lb. figs, chopped fine, three-fourths lb. bread crumbs, four oz. moist sugar (brown is best), one egg, well beaten, a little nutmeg, one c. of milk. Boil in a mould in thick bag four h.

SAUCE.—One c. sugar, two tbsp. butter, one egg and a champagne glass of wine. Beat yolk and white separately, the latter to a good froth; then mix in a bowl.

DESSERTS.

After boiling butter, sugar and wine together, pour over the eggs and return all to the saucepan and thicken for a moment over the fire. *Miss J. McC. Taylor.*

CUSTARD SOUFFLÉ

Two tbsp. butter, one-fourth c. flour, one c. heated milk, four eggs, one-fourth c. sugar. Mix butter, flour and hot milk same as white sauce. Pour this slowly over the well beaten yolks which have been mixed with the sugar. When this preparation is cool cut in the whites of the eggs which have been beaten to a stiff froth. Turn into a well buttered pudding dish and bake in very moderate oven from thirty to thirty-five m. When brown and well puffed serve at once with Foamy Sauce. Flavor pudding with vanilla.

CARAMEL CUSTARD.

Put one large pt. of milk in a farina boiler. Separate the yolks and whites of five eggs. Beat the yolks light and stir them into a scant pt. of cold milk, add the beaten whites of two eggs and partially sweeten. Take three large tbsp. of brown sugar and burn brown in a pie pan, stirring it while it burns. Stir this into the boiling milk and pour the hot milk gradually into cold milk and eggs. Then place in custard cups in a pan half full of water and set in oven. *Mrs. Jas. P. Speer.*

BAKED CUSTARD.

Five eggs to one qt. of milk, three whites left out. Warm half the milk, then add the other half, with the eggs well beaten. Add sugar and flavoring. Bake until stiff in a pan of water. *Mrs. E. M. Ferguson.*

DESSERTS.

THE PUTNAM THANKSGIVING PUDDING.

Take a loaf of stale bread, remove the crust and cut in thin slices. Spread thinly and very evenly with butter. Have a baking dish as near the size of two slices of bread laid *close* together as you can get. The less room outside the better. Lay the bread in the dish (*across* the dish) buttered side up; cover thickly and evenly with stoned raisins; then another layer of buttered bread as before; then raisins. Put the last layer buttered side down. Pour over it all the good rich milk that the dish will hold. Let it stand over night, covered with a plate or dish, and *weighted* down, so that the pudding will look like a "loaf." In the morning drain off all the milk and press the loaf to get it dry. Beat four eggs, perhaps a teacup of sugar, and a good deal of nutmeg; mix with the milk poured off, and pour over the pudding *slowly*, taking time for the loaf to absorb it. Bake about one h. Serve with hard sauce flavored with nutmeg. The pudding can be made with a meringue on top if desired but it was never done so in the old days.

GINGER PUDDING.

Two c. of flour, one-quarter of a c. of chopped suet, one-quarter of a c. of molasses, one-quarter of a c. of sugar, one-half of a tsp. of soda, two tsp. of ground ginger, one c. of milk, one-third of a tsp. of salt. Mix well together, turn into a greased mould and steam for four h. If in individual moulds three-quarters of an h. will be sufficient.

DANISH PUDDING.

Two c. brown sugar, eight eggs, one qt. milk, three c. water, two tbsp. vanilla. Heat the milk and add it to the eggs, which have been well beaten, stirring all the time. Burn the sugar in the skillet and add the three c. (or a little less) hot water. After the burnt sugar has been added to the milk and eggs, add the vanilla and bake in a moderate oven for 35 or 40 m. Place the porcelain pudding dish, in which the pudding is to bake, in a pan of water. After it is baked place the pudding in the refrigerator until the next day. Turn out and serve on flat dish. Surround pudding with whipped cream. *Mrs. Geo. A. Castleman.*

COCOANUT PUDDING.

Butter the size of an egg, three-fourths of a c. of sugar and one tbsp. of water. Boil a few m., then take from the fire, cool and add a c. and a half of grated cocoanut, the grated rind and juice of a lemon, the yolks of four eggs well beaten, one c. bread crumbs and a glass and a half of sherry wine. Last beat the whites of the eggs very light and place on top for meringue. Bake a short time in a moderate oven. *Miss J. McC. Taylor.*

PRUNE PUDDING.

Boil one lb. of prunes until they are swollen. Mash them through a colander. Beat with the prunes three tbsp. of pulverized sugar, then mix in the whites of six eggs, after having been beaten very light. Pour the mixture into bake dish and bake twenty m.

Mrs. Chase.

CREAM TAPIOCA PUDDING

Two tbsp. pearl tapioca, one pt. milk, yolks of two eggs, one-third c. sugar, one-eighth tsp. salt, whites of two eggs. Soak the tapioca in enough hot water to cover it, stirring until it absorbs some of the water, then

DESSERTS.

allow it to stand until the water is all absorbed; add the milk and cook until the tapioca is soft and transparent. Beat the yolks of the eggs and add the sugar and salt. Pour the milk over them and cook three m. Remove from the stove and add the whites of the eggs. Place in glass dish and allow to cool before serving with cream.

BAKED APPLE DUMPLINGS.

Make a short pie crust, roll it thin and cut it into squares large enough to cover an apple. Pare nice tart apples of same size, remove the core and fill spaces with sugar, butter and a little cinnamon, place an apple in center of each square, fold over carefully to keep juices in. Bake in moderate oven about forty m., brush the top with egg and dust a little sugar over and put back in oven a few m. Serve with hard sauce.

Mrs. H. S. Denny.

OATMEAL PUDDING.

Soak one and one-half c. of rolled oats on back of stove for one-half h. in a qt. of milk. Three eggs, whites and yolks beaten together, one and one-half c. of sugar, a pinch of salt, a little vanilla, one c. of raisins. Bake slowly one h. *Mrs. Albert H. Childs.*

INDIAN PUDDING.

Three pts. of boiled milk, two heaping tbsp. of corn meal. Boil these together for twenty m. Beat four eggs very light and add one c. of New Orleans molasses. One-half c. brown sugar, two and one-half tsp. of cinnamon, a little nutmeg and ground cloves, salt, butter the size of walnut. Bake in a *very* slow oven for four h.

Mrs. Albert H. Childs.

DESSERTS.

BREAD PUDDING.

One pt. bread crumbs. one-fourth tsp. salt, three eggs, one pt. milk. Soak the crumbs in cold water for one h. Wring the bread dry in a napkin and add the salt to the crumbs. Beat the eggs and add them to the milk. Then add the crumbs. Mix all with a fork Bake one h. in a well buttered dish. If a sweet liquid sauce is *not* used, two and a half tbsp. sugar must be added to the pudding. It is very nice served with cream.

BREAD AND APPLE PUDDING.

Place in a pudding dish a layer of stale bread which has been soaked in water till soft. All crust must be removed. Add four to six lumps of butter the size of a nutmeg, then a layer of stewed apples three-fourths of an inch thick. Sprinkle twenty or twenty-five seeded raisins over the apples and add another layer of bread, apples and rarsins, same as above. After baking in hot oven ten m., cover the top with a meringue made of whites of eggs and sugar. Reduce the heat of the oven and cook till brown. *L. W. Washington.*

FANCY APPLE PUDDING.

Pare six apples, take out cores and stew with sugar and lemon peel. Beat well four eggs, add one c. of bread crumbs, sugar and nutmeg. Butter a pudding dish, lay stewed apples in bottom of dish and cover with bread crumbs; put some small pieces of butter on top. Bake in quick oven. Turn upside down on flat dish; before serving sift powdered sugar over apples. Serve with whipped cream. *M. H.*

DESSERTS.

PEACH PUDDING.

Fill a pudding dish with whole peeled peaches and pour over them two c. of water. Cover closely and bake until the peaches are tender, then drain off the juice from the peaches and let it stand to cool. Add to the juice, when cool, one pt. of sweet milk, four well beaten eggs, a small c. of flour in which has been mixed one tsp. baking powder, one c. sugar, one tbsp. melted butter and a little salt. Beat thoroughly and pour over the peaches in the pudding dish. Bake until a rich brown and serve with cream.

HUCKLEBERRY PUDDING.

Three qts. berries, three tumblers flour, enough milk to wet the flour, if the water left from washing isn't enough. One tsp. salt. Put in a floured cloth and boil for three h. (in water boiling when dropped in). Serve with butter sauce.

SAUCE.—Two eggs, one c. sugar, one wine-glass wine. Beat well and long. *Mrs. Chauncey F. Black.*

BLUEBERRY PUDDING.

One qt. of berries, one qt. milk, one and one-half pts. stale bread, two eggs, one tsp. salt, one-fourth nutmeg, (grated), and four tbsp. sugar; soak the bread in the milk two h., then break up the bread with a spoon; beat the eggs, salt, sugar and nutmeg together, add this mixture to the bread and milk, then add the berries and bake in a slow oven for fifty m. *Mrs. H. S. Denny.*

ROLLY-POLY PUDDING.

Make a biscuit-dough, roll it out one-fourth inch thick, spread it with a little butter, sugar and any kind of berries, then roll it like a jelly roll, and tie it, and steam for one or two h. Serve with fruit sauce or cream.

Mrs. J. S. G.

BOILED INDIAN PUDDING.

Three c. corn meal, one c. beef suet, chopped fine, one c. molasses, a little salt, pour on boiling water enough to make a thick batter, beat well, now add three well beaten eggs, one tsp. cinnamon, one-half tsp. ginger, one-half c. stoned raisins, (these can be omitted if desired), two tsp. Royal baking powder. Steam four h.

May Breniser.

"OLD FASHIONED BOILED PUDDING."

"To make a pudding light as cake,
One qt. of cream you first must take,
(Or wanting that, good milk will do,
By adding butter thereunto):
Four eggs, and then four spoons of flour,
And boil it in a cloth an hour." *Mrs. Plitt.*

APPLE COMPOTE.

Golden gate, Wine Sap, or Pippin apples only, may be used for this recipe. Core and pare the apples, being careful not to break them. Boil the whole apples slowly in the following syrup, a few at a time (as each apple should be entirely immersed) until the apple is perfectly clear. To a qt. of water allow one pt. sugar and boil to a syrup before putting in the apples. It takes thirty to forty m. to cook the apples properly. After the apples are cooked and cold fill the center with marmalade—orange or strawberry preferred—place them in a glass dish and pour a little of the cold syrup around them. *L. W. Washington.*

DESSERTS.

TO MAKE JELLY FROM FEET.

Boil four calf's feet that have been nicely cleaned and the hoof's taken off. When the feet are boiled to pieces, strain the liquor through a colander, and when cold, take all the grease off, and put the jelly in a skillet, leaving the dregs, which will be at the bottom. There should be from four feet, about two qts. of jelly. Pour into it one qt. of white wine, the juice of six fresh lemons strained from the seeds, one lb. and a half of powdered loaf sugar, a little pounded cinnamon, and mace, and the rind thinly pared from two of the lemons. Wash eight eggs very clean, whip up the whites to a very light froth, crush the shells and put with them, mix with the jelly and set it on the fire, stirring occasionally till the jelly is melted, but do not touch it afterwards. When it has boiled until it looks quite clear on one side, and the dross accumulates on the other, take off carefully the thickest part of the dross, and pour the jelly in the bag; put back in the bag what runs through until it becomes quite transparent, then set a pitcher under the bag, and put a cover all over to keep out the dust. The jelly looks much prettier when it is broken to fill the glasses. The bag should be made of cotton or linen, and be suspended in a frame (jelly strainer) made for the purpose. The feet of hogs make the palest colored jelly; those of sheep are a beautiful amber color, when prepared. If the jelly bag is thin, take off less of the dross.

The feet, after the stock is made, are good fried and seasoned with pepper and salt. *Mrs. Randolph.*

DESSERTS.

BOILED JELLY.

One package gelatin, one pt. cold water, let stand one-half h., then add one pt. boiling water and stir until the gelatin entirely dissolves. Add one and one-half pts. pale sherry wine, four sticks cinnamon, six large blades mace, three lemons, one doz. fine raisins. Sweeten to taste. Beat the white of one egg stiff, mix it with the jelly and stir until the mixture is very hot. Then simmer, without stirring, until the egg looks brown and curdled and the jelly is clear. Strain through flannel bag which has been scalded. *Mrs. J. B. Washington.*

WINE JELLY.

One package Keystone Silver White gelatin, one-half c. cold water, one pt. boiling water, one c. sugar, one lemon, one c. wine. Very nice jelly is made by using one-half c. brandy and one-half c. sherry. Soak gelatin in cold water until soft; add the boiling water and the sugar. Stir until the sugar is dissolved, then add the lemon juice, and when cooled, the wine. Strain through a flannel bag or through cheese cloth placed in a wire sieve. Harden jelly by placing it near the ice.

COFFEE JELLY.

One-fourth pack Keystone Silver White gelatin, one-half c. sugar, three tbsp. brandy, one and one-half c. cold water, two c. strong hot coffee. Use directions for mixing wine jelly.

JELLIED PRUNES.

One pt. of prunes, one and one-half pt. of water, one-half a package of Keystone Silver White gelatin, one-half pt. of wine, and one-half pt. of sugar. Soak the

DESSERTS.

gelatin in one gill of the water for two hours. Wash the prunes well and cook slowly for one h. in the rest of the water. Take out the prunes and remove the stones. Return to the water in the stew pan and let boil up. Add the gelatin and take from the fire. Stir until the gelatin is dissolved, then add sugar and wine and place the stew pan in a pan of ice water, stirring until the preparation begins to thicken. Pour into moulds and set in cool place for four or five h. to harden. Serve with soft custard or whipped cream.

BLANC MANGE.

One oz. of Russian isinglass to one qt. of cream, sweeten to the taste (a little sweet), stir it well all the time on the fire, strain through thin muslin. When the moulds are scalded and made cold, dip it into them with a spoon. It should boil two or three m. One-half c. of rose water to one qt. of cream. *Mrs. Johnston.*

BLANC MANGE.

One pt. of cream, one pt. of new milk, one-third box of gelatin, one tbsp. of sugar, one tsp. of vanilla. Soak the gelatin in the milk until dissolved, then add the sugar, put it in a double boiler until thoroughly heated, then take it off and strain through a strainer, when cool add the cream and vanilla, stir it to keep it from getting lumpy and when the consistency of thick cream, put in a mould. *Mrs. E. M. Ferguson.*

CREAM BLANC MANGE

One qt. cream heated to boiling point. Soak one-half package gelatin in cold watter, pour the hot cream over it, sweeten and flavor to taste with bitter almond.

Mrs. Keyser.

DESSERTS.

CHOCOLATE BLANC MANGE.

Four squares Baker's chocolate, six tbsp. granulated sugar, and a little water. Boil this one and one-half h. Boil almost three pts. milk and add the chocolate and one-half pack of gelatine soaked in *cold* water. Cook just five m. stirring all the time and then pour into moulds. *Mrs. Keyser.*

VELVET CREAM.

Thicken a pt. of milk with one-half a box of gelatin, let it melt in the heated milk. When the milk is cool add to it a pt. of cream which has been sweetened and flavored to taste. Pour it in to moulds and set on ice to stiffen. *Miss J. McC. Taylor*

MRS SHIPMAN'S CREAM

One pt. cream whipped to stiff froth, one-half box gelatin soaked in a little water, one pine-apple cut into small pieces and simmered until soft with a coffee c. of sugar. Strain the pine-apple through a colander into the gelatin, and, when quite cold, stir the cream thoroughly into it. Put in a mould on ice. Peaches may be used in the same way. *Mrs. Moore.*

CHARLOTTE RUSSE.

Dissolve one-half a box of Cox's sparkling gelatin in one pt. milk. When it boils pour it on the yolks of two eggs, well beaten ; add one-half lb. sugar and either essence of vanilla or bitter almond. Stir it occasionally till it begins to thicken, then add the whites of five eggs, beaten to a stiff froth, then one pt. very rich cream, whipped to a stiff froth. Line the bottom and sides of four moulds with lady fingers and fill with the Charlotte.

DESSERTS.

If the weather is mild put it on ice. Before turning out the moulds trim the edges of the cake smooth that it may set well on the plates or dishes. *Mrs. Hugh Lee.*

CHARLOTTE RUSSE.

One qt. cream, six eggs, six tbsp. sugar, two-thirds box gelatin, one-half c. water, two wine glasses sherry. Dissolve the gelatin in the water; whip the yolks and sugar; whip the whites to a stiff froth and add to the yolks. Then add the cream and last the gelatin. Whip until it congeals. *Mrs. Whiting.*

INVALID'S CHARLOTTE RUSSE.

To a pt. of rich milk add one-half package of gelatin which has been dissolved in one c. cold water, the whites of two eggs well beaten, one tbsp. sugar and one-half tsp. vanilla or bitter almond to taste. Pour this over lady fingers or sponge cake, which has been steeped in sherry wine and placed in the bottom and on the sides of a glass dish. Set in a cold place until firm. This is very nice served with a soft custard used as a sauce.
Mrs. J. B. Washington.

STRAWBERRY SHORT CAKE.

One qt. flour, one-half c. pulverized sugar, three tsp. of baking powder, a pinch of salt. Sift all together, then rub in butter the size of two eggs. Beat one egg well in a cup and add milk enough to egg to moisten. Do not make dough too soft, and when adding milk and egg stir lightly with a fork. Roll thin and bake in well floured cake pans. *Mrs. Wm. H. Singer, Jr.*

DESSERTS.

STRAWBERRY CHARLOTTE.

Cut large firm strawberries in two lengthwise; dip them in liquid gelatin, and line a plain mould, placing the flat side against the mould; if the mould is set on ice the gelatin will harden at once and hold the berries in place; fill the center with charlotte filling made by whipping one pt. of cream to stiff froth, soak half oz. of gelatin in three tbsp. cold water for half h., then dissolve it with two tbsp. boiling water; add to the whipped cream a tbsp. powdered sugar and two dessert-spoonfuls of any liquor or a tsp. of vanilla; then turn in slowly the dissolved gelatin, beating all the time, when it begins to stiffen turn into the mould lined with berries.

M. I. H.

PEACH SPONGE.

Six large, ripe, juicy peaches, one-half box gelatin, one c. of sugar, whites of two eggs. put peaches through a sieve, and let all come to a boil, when cold add the eggs beaten to a stiff froth. One can of peaches may be used in place of ripe ones. *Mrs. W. A. Peterson.*

RICE MERANGUE PUDDING.

Boil one c. rice in water, when water boils away, add one pt. milk, a piece of butter size of walnut, yolks of two eggs, one-half c. sugar, flavoring to taste, mix well, pour into pudding dish. Spread over the top a merangue of the whites of the eggs and brown in oven.

STRAWBERRY MERANGUE.

Whites of seven eggs, seven tbsp. powdered sugar, one-half tsp. salt, one-half c. strawberry preserve; beat the eggs to stiff froth, then with a spoon gradually beat

DESSERTS, 115

the sugar and salt into the froth ; butter a dish and drop spoonfuls of the meringue upon the bottom of the dish, and half spoonfuls of the preserve, continue until both are used. Bake in a moderate oven twenty-five m. Serve very cold with whipped cream.

Mrs. H. S. Denny.

MERANGUE.

One box of gelatin, nine eggs, three pts. milk, one tumbler of wine, vanilla to flavor. Soak the gelatin in the milk about twenty m.; put it on the fire, and, when it boils, stir quickly in the yolks of the eggs, which have been beaten with one-half lb. sugar; stir until it thickens; remove from the fire and stir in the whites, which have been beaten to a *stiff froth*, with a c. of sugar. Flavor well with vanilla, and add a tumbler of wine. Stir just to mix, and pour as quickly as possible into the moulds. If properly made there will be two or three inches of clear jelly in the bottom of each mould. Make several h. before it is wanted. I always make it the day before.

Emily Baker.

BOILED CUSTARD.

Yolks of one doz. eggs to one full qt. of fresh milk, one vanilla bean, sugar to taste. Put the milk on to boil with the vanilla bean in it, stirring it frequently to prevent its burning. Beat the eggs well and pour the milk boiling hot on them, stirring them well together; add powdered sugar enough to make it quite sweet. Let the kettle in which the milk was boiled be quite clean, and put the custard back into it. Put it on the fire and stir it without cessation until it thickens. It must not boil, only thicken. If left too long it will curdle ; if not long enough it will be too thin. It should be watched most carefully. Should it curdle place the vessel in which it has been cooked in a basin of cold water and beat vigorously with Dover egg beater, when the custard will become quite smooth again. It makes a very nice dish to soak macaroons in wine and pour this custard over them. The whites of the eggs may also be used as a merangue. *Mrs. H. L. Johnston.*

FRIED BANANAS.

Cut in slices lengthwise, drop in egg and then in sugar and flour mixed; fry in lard until brown and serve hot.
Mrs. H. S. Denny.

BATTER FOR FRUIT FRITTERS.

One c. of flour, half a c. of milk, two eggs, one tbsp. of sugar, one tbsp. of melted butter, half a tsp. of salt and the yellow rind of one-fourth of a lemon grated.
Mrs. H. S. Denny.

APPLE FRITTERS.

Pare and core six large tart apples; cut in slices one-third of an inch thick and lay them in a bowl over which sprinkle three tbsp. of sugar, one-fourth of a grated nutmeg and the juice of one lemon. Let them stand for half an h. or more and then dip the slices into the fruit batter and drop into hot fat, and cook three m. Drain and serve on flat dish, sift powdered sugar over the slices. Peach, pear, pineapple and banana fritters can be made the same way. *Mrs. H. S. Denny.*

DESSERTS. 117

MINCE MEAT.

One lb. of lean beef, boiled and chopped fine, one-half lb. raisins (the best raisins, seeded and cut), two lbs. currants, two lbs. suet shredded, one lb. citron, sliced thin, two lbs. good brown sugar, eight lbs. Pippin apples, two lemons (grated rinds) and the juice of one-half of one of them, two nutmegs grated, one tsp. powdered mace, a pinch of powdered cloves, one qt. or a little more wine, one pt. brandy, rum, or whiskey. This quantity makes fifteen pies. Keep in a cool place.

Mrs. Perine.

MINCE MEAT.

Three lbs. boiled beef, chopped fine, two lbs. suet, chopped fine, three lbs. raisins, three lbs. currants, five lbs. chopped apples, one lb. citron, cut fine, one nutmeg, two tbsp. ground cinnamon, one tsp. cloves, one tsp. allspice, one-half tsp. mace, one tbsp. salt, three lbs. brown sugar, and two qts. rum or brandy. *Mrs. H. P. Allen.*

PUMPKIN PUDDING OR PIE.

To three pts. of pumpkin after it is well stewed and squeezed, add one-fourth lb. of butter, eight eggs well beaten, one-half pt. of cream, the same of milk, one wine glass of brandy and wine mixed, cinnamon, sugar and nutmeg to taste. Bake for three-fourths of an h.

Miss Kerfoot.

APPLE PIE.

Receipt for two large pies. Three qts. of pared and sliced apples, two c. of sugar, one-third of a nutmeg grated, two tbsp. of flour and eight of water. Cover two deep plates with your paste, then divide the apples equally, putting half in each plate. Mix sugar, flour and nutmeg and sprinkle half over each pie then sprinkle four tbsp. of water over each pie. Cover with paste and bake in a moderate oven fifty m. If one does not care for a very deep pie, the same receipt can be used making the pies smaller. *Mrs. H. S Denny.*

LEMON PIES.

Yolks of five eggs, white of one egg, one and one-half coffee c. sugar, one good spoonful of butter, melted, five heaping spoonfuls sifted flour mixed with sugar and eggs. Juice and rind of four lemons. Sufficient water with lemon juice to make one and one-half tea c.
Mrs. Whiting.

TYLERS.

Three eggs, one-half c. melted butter, two c. sugar, one c. sweet milk, the grated rind and juice of one lemon. Bake on nice pastry in pastry pans. This quantity will make twelve tartlets. *Mrs. J. B. Washington.*

TRANSPARENT PIES.

Eight eggs, one lb. granulated sugar, two-thirds lb. butter, two lemons, rind and juice. Beat the yolk of the eggs and sugar together until very light. Melt the butter and beat into the eggs and sugar. Add the lemon juice and the grated rind. Beat the whites of four eggs and add last. Bake in pie crust in a moderate oven. Whip the remaining whites and add one tbsp. sugar to each egg and meringue the pies.
Mrs. J. B. Washington.

DESSERTS.

TRANSPARENT PUDDING.

Four coffee c. confectioners' sugar, five eggs, one and one-half c. butter and one nutmeg. Beat the butter and sugar together, and add the eggs, one at a time; add the nutmeg and mix thoroughly. Place the bowl containing this mixture in a pan of hot water and warm through, stirring constantly. Put in pie pans lined with pastry and bake in rather slow oven.

Mrs. George A. Castleman.

WASHINGTON PIE.

One c. sugar, three eggs—beaten separately, two tbsp. cold water, small pinch salt, one c. flour, and two tbsp. baking powder. Bake in deep jelly cake pans and when cool cut open and fill with the following mixture. Mix two eggs, two heaping tbsp. sugar and one tbsp. flour thoroughly together and stir them into one pt. hot milk. Stir vigorously and constantly while it cooks to keep the custard quite smooth, and when cool flavor with lemon, almond or vanilla. *Mrs. H. P. Allen.*

DESSERTS.

SAUCES.

FOR FISH.

WHITE SAUCE FOR FISH.

Make cream sauce, and to two c. sauce add one-half tbsp. lemon juice and three or four olives chopped fine.

CUCUMBER SAUCE.

Make some highly seasoned and very stiff mayonnaise. Pare several cucumbers, according to the quantity of sauce you require. After the cucumbers have soaked in salted ice water for several h., slice them about one-fourth of an inch thick, and cut into small dice. Dry the chopped cucumbers several times *very thoroughly* (between cloths) and just before serving mix with the mayonnaise and add some capers. The mayonnaise should be thick, or the water in the cucumbers will make the sauce too thin.

Miss M. C. Speer.

SAUCES.
FOR MEATS.

CHIVES SAUCE.

Put a c. of bread crumbs in a saucepan with two oz. butter and stir until a pale golden brown, then pour in one-half pt. broth with two tbsp. of finely chopped chives and season to taste. Stir the sauce over the fire till boiling and keep very smooth.

LEMON SAUCE FOR BOILED FOWL.

Peel a large lemon, cut in slices. Pick out all the pips and cut the slices into small pieces. Boil a fowl's liver, then chop and add it to the lemon, pour one-half pt. hot melted butter over and serve it in a sauce boat with the fowl.

BROWN SAUCE.

Flour well two sliced onions and put in skillet with about dessert spoonful of hot lard and four tomatos, cut up, and let all brown well *without frying*, then add meat, chicken, veal or anything you wish to cook, and let all cook slowly. Add a little hot water occasionally if the gravy gets too thick. Season with salt, red and black pepper, and when finished, ready to serve, scatter over very finely chopped parsley. Flour meat well before putting in skillet. This sauce is good for anything. Fish sliced and cooked in it, the slices put on toast and the gravy put over it, you will find delicious. You can, also, in cooking duck, add carrots and turnips. A great improvement. *Mrs. Wm. H. Singer, Jr.*

SAUCES.

PAPILOTTE SAUCE.

Chop fine two onions, put them into a stewpan, with one-half oz. scraped fat of bacon, and stir over the fire for five m.; then pour in one pt. brown sauce. When boiling add one tbsp. chopped parsley and mushrooms, a small quantity scraped garlic, a lump of sugar, a little nutmeg and pepper, and salt to taste. Stir constantly and boil till reduced to a creamy thickness, then remove from fire and set aside to cool. Generally served with cutlets à la maintenon.

FOR VEGETABLES.

CREAM OR WHITE SAUCE.

Two tbsp. butter, two tbsp. flour, one tsp. salt, one pt. milk (hot), one-eighth tsp. pepper. Heat the butter until it bubbles: add the flour and salt, and gradually the hot milk. If used for vegetables add the pepper. If it lumps, cook until it thickens, then beat until it is smooth. It may be removed from the fire and beaten. A thicker sauce than this receipt will make, requires less milk. A thinner sauce requires more milk. A richer sauce requires cream or white stock. The butter and flour must be browned for brown sauce.

WHITE SAUCE, OR DRAWN BUTTER, FOR VEGETABLES.

One c. hot milk, one c. vegetable stock (water in which vegetables have been cooked), two tbsp butter, one and one-half tbsp. flour, salt and pepper. Melt the butter and add the flour and seasoning. Then add gradually the hot milk and stock, cook five m. and pour over the vegetable to be served.

WHITE SAUCE.

Enough for a cauliflower or one pair chickens. Take the yolks of six eggs, beat them as light as possible. Take about one-fourth lb. or little more butter and let it melt in a saucepan on the fire, add a pinch of salt to the melted butter. Have some one else place cauliflower or chicken or sweetbread in a very hot dish, and while that is being done pour the egg into the butter, stirring all the time. Give it a quick stir after all is in and pour at once on the dish to be served. A little lemon can be squeezed in at the table, or if the sauce curdles, pour it back into the saucepan, squeeze a little lemon into it and give it a stir. *Mrs. Berghmans.*

FOR DESSERT.

DEVONSHIRE CREAM.

Put fresh milk on the fire and let it very slowly come to scalding point, but do not let it boil, leave it on the fire for about half an h. Then remove to a cold place and let it stand for six h. or until the cream has all risen. It will be thick and clotted and is nice on fruits, mush, etc. It will keep for some time and is much better than plain cream. *M. I. H.*

SAUCES.

CREAM SAUCE.

One-half c. of butter, one c. of sugar, the yolk of one egg. Beat together to a cream, then beat in quickly a wineglass full of sherry ; add two tbsp. of boiling water ; beat this all thoroughly, then add the well beaten white of the egg. The secret of this sauce is in the beating.

Mrs. J. H. Shoenberger.

CREAMY SAUCE.

One egg, one c. powdered sugar, one-half c. thick cream, one-fourth c. milk, one-half tsp. vanilla. Beat white of egg until stiff, add well beaten yolk and gradually the sugar, If the cream is too thick dilute with the milk and beat until stiff. Combine the two mixtures and flavor.

FOAMY SAUCE.

Whites of two eggs, one c. pulverized sugar, one-fourth c. hot milk, one tsp. vanilla, sherry or brandy. Beat whites until stiff and dry, add sugar gradually and continue to beat. Add hot milk gradually, then the flavoring and serve.

This sauce is best if made not longer than an h. before serving.

WINE SAUCE FOR PLUM PUDDING.

One-half pt. of sherry, one-half lb. of sifted sugar, about two oz. of butter, a little nutmeg. Stir it over the fire until the sugar is all dissolved. Let it simmer a few m., but do not let it come to a boil.

Mrs. T. C. Carroll.

SAUCES.

SAUCE FOR THE PLUM PUDDING OR ANY OTHER BOILED OR BAKED PUDDING.

One-half lb. butter, eight tbsp. of nice brown sugar, one nutmeg, the white of an egg, a wineglass of wine. The butter must be creamed and the sugar beaten with it; then the egg, the wine poured in gently and stirred until it is cold. It is best to mix it in a common bowl on the hearth stirring it all the time—it must not boil. It is soon made and ought to look *as thick as salad dressing*. *Mrs. Nicholson.*

WINE SAUCE.

One c. butter and one c. pulverized sugar beaten to a light thick cream. To this add gradually a wineglass of boiling water, a large wineglass of the best brandy, a small nutmeg, grated, and the juice and grated rind of a large lemon or orange. It is well to mix this sauce in an earthenware bowl set in a pan of hot water.

WINE SAUCE.

Yolks of two eggs, one-eighth lb. butter, four tbsp. brown sugar, nutmeg, and three wineglasses of wine—more if you like it very strong. Mix all together; put the vessel in a pan of hot water to boil quite thick, stirring constantly. *Mrs. H. P. Allen.*

LEMON SAUCE.

Three-fourths c. sugar, one-half c. butter, one egg, juice and half the grated rind of a lemon, one tsp. nutmeg, and one-half c. boiling water. Cream the butter and sugar, and beat in the egg, whipped very light; add lemon and nutmeg. Beat hard, then add the water;

SAUCES.

put in a tin pail and set within the uncovered top of the teakettle, which must boil until the sauce is very hot, but not boiling. Stir constantly.

HOT CHOCOLATE SAUCE.

One and one-half c. pulverized sugar, butter the size of an egg, one-half cake (or one-fourth lb.) Baker's chocolate, one c. cream, one-fourth c. sherry, and one tsp. vanilla. Thoroughly mix the butter, sugar and grated chocolate; add the cream and boil for six or seven m. Stir in the flavoring, and after it has cooked a few seconds longer, it is ready to serve. This sauce is intended for vanilla ice cream, and should be served very hot.

Mrs. Thomas M. Jones, Jr.

HARD SAUCE.

One-half c. of butter, well beaten, stir in slowly one c. of fine sugar, and beat to a cream. Flavor with one tbsp. sherry or brandy. Pile on a plate and grate over it a little nutmeg. Keep on ice till ready to serve.

SAUCES.

CAKE.

SUGGESTIONS ON CAKE BAKING.

Always use lard to grease your cake pans as the salt in butter causes the cake to stick to the pans. Whites of eggs will froth quicker if you add a pinch of salt. Always cream the butter and sugar first, then add the yolks of the eggs, then milk and last the flour and whites of eggs. To one qt. of flour use two and one-half tsp. of Royal baking powder, one tsp. of soda and two of cream of tartar. Cake should always be beaten, not stirred. If a cake is too solid put in a few tsp. of milk and if too soft add a tbsp. or more of flour. Keep the oven closed at least ten m. after putting in your cake. Cover the bottoms of your cake pans with plain white or manilla paper. Never try to ice a cake while hot. A bowl or pan containing water set in an oven when baking will prevent pies or cakes from scorching.

A VERY GOOD LUNCH CAKE.

One-half lb. butter, four c. sugar, eight eggs, six c. flour, three tsp. soda, four tsp. cream of tartar, two c. of sweet milk. Cream the butter, add the sugar (beat the eggs separately), add the yolks to the butter, add the milk with the soda in it, then the flour with the cream of tartar in it alternately with the whites of the eggs. Bake about twenty m. Do not put much in the flat pans, one and one-half inch enough. Flavor with nutmeg, or nutmeg and brandy, or rose water, or the rind of lemon, grated fine. *Mrs. H. L. Johnston.*

LADY CAKE.

One c. butter, one c. sugar, whites of eight eggs, one c. sweet cream, three c. flour, three tsp. yeast powder, sifted in the dry flour, and one dessert spoonful almond extract Cream butter and sugar together; add cream, then the flour, and last thing the flavoring and the whites of the eggs beaten very stiff. Bake in a quick oven in two bread pans If desired this cake may be iced with plain boiled icing flavored with almond extract.
"*Cloud Capped.*"

SPONGE CAKE.

Take any even number of eggs and weigh the sugar with them. Take one-half the eggs—using the largest ones—and weigh the flour with them. Beat the yolks and sugar together thoroughly. Sift the flour in gradually, and add lemon juice and grated lemon rind from time to time. Last cut in the whites of the eggs beaten very light. Bake in a moderate and very even oven.
"*Cloud Capped.*"

SPONGE CAKE.

Ten eggs, one lb. sugar, one-half lb. sifted flour, one lemon. Beat sugar and yolks of eggs together. Grate in the rind of one lemon, then add the whites of the eggs well beaten. Add the flour last and do not beat after the flour is in. *Mrs. E. M. Ferguson.*

CAKE.

ANGEL FOOD.

Whites of twenty-two eggs beaten to a stiff froth; two tumblers of flour, sifted five times, three tumblers of fine granulated sugar, sifted four times, four tsp. of vanilla, two tsp. cream tartar. Beat sugar into eggs, measure flour again after last sifting to make sure, mix in the cream of tartar, and sift all again into eggs, stirring with utmost gentleness; add vanilla and bake immediately in a pan which has never been greased. Put wet papers in the bottom and sides. Bake forty m. in a *moderate oven.* When done, turn the pan upside down on a sifter and leave until perfectly cold. *Mrs. R. S. Albert.*

FEATHER CAKE.

One c. white sugar, one c. of sweet milk, one and one-half c. flour, one tbsp. of butter, three tsp. of Royal baking powder, one egg, flavor to taste.

Mrs. J. H. Murdock.

CORN STARCH CAKE.

Two c. white sugar, three-fourths c. of butter, one c. of milk, one c. of corn starch, two c. of sifted flour, the whites of seven eggs, a tbsp. of Royal baking powder. Let the oven be hot, but not too hot, or it will rise before baking. *Miss Mary K. Snyder.*

CUP CAKE.

Six eggs, six c. of flour, one lb. brown sugar, three c. of melted butter, one c. of cream, one and one-half c. of molasses, two nutmegs, one tsp. of soda, dissolved in a little cream. First beat the eggs, adding the sugar by spoonsful; then put in the cream, then the butter by small quantities, then molasses and nutmeg; mix in each ingredient well; stir in the flour, and lastly the soda. Bake immediately. This is a delicious cake.

Mrs. Joseph White.

GEN. LEE CAKE.

Ten eggs, one lb. pulverized sugar, the rinds of one or two lemons and the juice of one, one-half lb. flour. Beat the whites and yolks of the eggs separately very light. To the yolks add the sugar, the rinds, the juice of the lemons, the whites of the eggs, then the flour, stirring each ingredient slowly as added. Bake in jelly pans in a quick oven, first greasing the pans with butter. When turned out to cool put the icing between, and on top of the layers. *Mrs. H. L Johnston.*

INDIAN MEAL CAKE.

One lb. sugar, one lb. corn meal (take out one handful of meal and put in its place one handful of flour), four eggs; one-half lb. butter, one nutmeg, cinnamon to taste, a little rose water. *Miss Loulie Macgill.*

PISTACHIO CAKE.

Sift one c. of flour three times before measuring and twice afterwards. Pour four tbsp of boiling water over one c. of sugar, set over the fire until dissolved, then cool ; to the prepared flour add one and one-half tsp. of salt. Blanch two ounces of pistachio nuts, pound to a paste, then press through a sieve. Mix all these ingredients together, add the stiffly beaten whites of four eggs and ten drops of vanilla and beat steadily for ten m. Turn into a greased pan and bake half an h. in a moderate oven.

CAKE. 141

FRUIT CAKE.

Two lbs. raisins *stoned*, one lb. citron, two lbs. currants, twelve eggs, one lb. butter, one lb. sugar, one lb. *heavy* flour, wineglass and a half of brandy, two nutmegs, three tsp. of cinnamon, one tsp. of cloves. Put the fruit into the flour; cream the butter and sugar, and beat the yolks of the eggs very light and *with the hand ;* beat and cream them all together; then add brandy and spices, putting the spices in the brandy, then the whites, well beaten, after which directly add fruit and flour. Bake two or three h., putting paper in the pan *under* the cake, and, when it commences to brown, put white paper over the cake,

Mrs. Dunbar's Receipt from Letitia Davis.

To Make Black Cake.

Add a c. of molasses to the brandy and spices, and make as above. *Mrs. H. L. Johnston.*

FRUIT CAKE.

One lb. butter, one lb. sugar, twelve eggs, one lb. flour, three lbs. raisins, three lbs. currants, one lb. citron, one c. molasses, one tbsp. ground cloves, one tbsp. cinnamon, one tbsp. mace or nutmeg, one wineglass full brandy, one wineglass full sherry. Use one-third of the flour to roll the fruit in. Cream the butter as lightly as possible; add the sugar and beat well together, then add the well beaten yolks and beat hard again. Now add the molasses, then the stiffly beaten whites of the eggs, then the spices, fruit, flour and brandy. Be very careful to rub the fruit well with the flour or it will sink to the bottom of the cake. Bake in a moderate but steady oven three or four h. *Mrs. Chauncey F. Black.*

FRUIT CAKE.

One lb. butter, one lb. sugar, twelve eggs, one lb. flour, dried and sifted, one tbsp. of the following spices mixed: cloves, cinnamon, nutmeg and mace. A smaller proportion of the mace than of the others. Two wineglasses of rose water, two wineglasses of brandy, three lbs. raisins well floured, three-fourths lb. currants well washed, dried and floured, one-fourth lb. citron and one-half lb. blanched almonds. Beat eggs separately. Cream, butter and sugar together and add yolks of eggs. Then add alternately the flour and whites of eggs, then the rose water, brandy and spices, and the currants and raisins. Line the cake pan with well greased paper and put in alternate layers of batter and citron and almonds. Bake for four h. in a steady oven. *Miss Jennie McC Taylor.*

FRUIT CAKE.

Thirty-five eggs, three lbs. flour, three lbs. sugar, two lbs. butter, ten lbs. raisins, six lbs. currants, five lbs. citron, six tbsp. of cinnamon, six tbsp. of mace, four tbsp. of cloves, three wineglasses wine, three wineglasses brandy, one lemon, one orange, one tsp. soda. Brown and sift part of the flour. *Mrs. E. M. Ferguson.*

FRUIT CAKE.

One lb. of sugar, one lb. of butter, three lbs. of currants, three lbs. of raisins, one lb. of citron, ten eggs, one lb. of flour, one wineglass of brandy, one tumbler of molasses, nutmeg, cinnamon, mace.
Mrs. Byron H. Painter.

CAKE. 143

MOCHA CAKES, No. 1.

Cream one c. of butter and beat into it gradually one c. of sugar. When very light and creamy add alternately five eggs well beaten and two c. sifted flour. Stir in two tbsp. of sherry and two tbsp. of brandy, then beat hard for at least ten m. Butter straight-sided moulds three inches in diameter, half fill with the batter and bake in a moderate oven; or bake in a sheet three inches thick and stamp out with a three-inch cutter. When cold split the cake in half-inch layers, spread with the filling and put three layers together. Put a little of the filling on the sides and roll in desiccated cocoanut. Put the remainder of the filling in a pastry bag with a small rose tube and press out on the top of the cake.

Filling for Mocha Cakes

Wash one-half of a c. of butter and cream gradually with one c. of powdered sugar. When very creamy add one c. of cream filling made by scalding one c. of milk and adding to it one egg, one-third of a c. of sugar, one scant fourth of a c. of flour and a pinch of salt beaten together ; cook until thick and flavor with strong black coffee, then set away until cold. Beat all together well and keep in a cold place until used.

MOCHA CAKES No. 2.

Four eggs, the weight of the eggs in sugar, one-half of the weight of the eggs in flour, the grated rind of one lemon. Beat the yolks of the eggs and the sugar together until very light and creamy, add the rind of the lemon and one-half of the flour. Beat the whites to a stiff froth, add half of them to the mixture, then the remainder of the flour, and lastly the remainder of the whites. Pour into a greased cake pan, making the batter about one-half of an inch thick. Bake in a moderate oven and when cold cut in three-inch circles. From one-half of these circles cut the center, leaving rings which should be fastened to the uncut circles with a little white of egg. In the c. thus formed put the following cream filling:

One pt. of thick cream whipped to a stiff froth, one-third of a c. of powdered sugar, sufficient very strong black coffee to flavor.

CARAMEL CAKE.

One even c butter, two even c. sugar, three even c. of flour, whites eight eggs, two even tsp. baking powder, one tsp. vanilla, one c. milk. Stir sugar and butter to a cream, add milk slowly, then flour in which baking powder has been mixed, then the well beaten whites of the eggs, and vanilla. Bake in layer tins, with well greased paper lining each one.

For the Caramel Icing.

Two c. brown sugar, one c. cream, three tbsp. butter, one tsp. vanilla. Boil all the ingredients, except the vanilla, until it will hold together in cold water. Then add the vanilla. If it should curdle, strain and boil again. Spread between and on tops of layers.

Mrs. Jere S. Black.

ORANGE CAKE.

Three eggs beaten separately, one coffee c. sugar, one coffee c. flour (heaping), four tbsp. cold water, two level tsp. yeast powder, season with orange. Cook in layers in quick oven.

CAKE. 145

Filling.

Grated rind of one orange, juice of two oranges, one coffee c. sugar, one coffee c. boiling water, three tbsp. corn starch. Put on in sauce pan and let thicken to a jelly. Spread this between the layers of the cake and sprinkle top of cake with pulverized sugar. This cake is better if it is made the day before it is to be eaten.

Miss Bena L. Coleman.

CHOCOLATE CAKE.

Three eggs, beaten separately, one coffee c. sugar, one coffee c. flour, heaping, one c. milk, three tbsp. melted butter, two level tsp. yeast powder. Season with vanilla. Cook in layers in quick oven.

Filling.

Three squares of chocolate, one large tbsp. of butter, one c. sugar, one egg, one-half c. hot water. Season with vanilla. Put chocolate and butter on to melt them. Put in the sugar, mix well, break egg into this mixture and add hot water slowly so as not to cook the egg. Cook about ten or fifteen m. and then add the vanilla.

Miss Bena L. Coleman.

PLAIN CAKE.

One c. butter, two c. sugar, three c. flour, four eggs; dissolve one tsp. soda in a c. milk and sift two tsp. cream of tartar through the flour. Flavor with vanilla or bitter almond.

PLAIN CAKE.

Four eggs beaten very light separately, two c. even full granulated sugar beaten with the yolks, two-thirds c. melted butter, added next; three even c. sifted flour, three even tsp. baking powder sifted with the flour, two-thirds c. milk added by degrees with the flour to the eggs and sugar. Flavor with the rind and juice of a large lemon. *Mrs. Thomas H. Dickson.*

PLAIN CAKE.

Four eggs, two even c. sifted flour, one full tsp. baking powder, sifted with the flour, one c. sweet cream, one full tea c. granulated sugar, one lemon rind grated and one-half the juice. Beat the yolks of eggs and sugar very light; add the cream, lemon and the flour by degrees. Last the whites beaten very light.
Mrs. J. B. Washington.

LEMON JELLY CAKE.

Make any plain cake, bake in layers and put together with the following filling :

One-half lb. butter, one-half lb. sugar, six eggs, six lemons. Cook until stiff as jelly. *Miss Commack.*

BOILED ICING.

Boil one c. of granulated sugar with four tbsp. water until it drops from the spoon in a thread ; have ready the beaten white of one egg, and pour the syrup slowly into it beating all the time ; flavor and spread on cake while warm. *Anna Marker.*

MAPLE SUGAR ICING.

One c. maple sugar, one and a half c. brown sugar, one half c. butter, three-fourths c. milk. Boil together until it shreds off spoon, then add one heaping c. of pecan nuts, chopped, and vanilla to flavor.
Miss Sallie Black, Greensburg.

CAKE.

MARSHMALLOW FILLING.

Soak two oz. of pure gum-arabic in half a c. of warm water for half an h. then add one-half c. of boiling water and put it into a double boiler; add a half lb. of powdered sugar, stir over the fire for twenty m.; then add a tbsp. of soaked gelatin. Beat the whites of two eggs to a stiff froth, pour the hot mixture over them slowly, then beat for fifteen m. or until perfectly cool. Your cake must be cold before the filling is put between the layers.

PLAIN ICING.

Place the white of an egg on a plate, add a little lemon juice or orange or any flavoring and a few drops of water. Stir in powdered sugar until it is thick enough to spread. While the cake is yet warm pile the icing in the center and with a wet knife smooth it over the top and sides. It will settle into a smooth glossy surface. One egg will take about a c. of sugar and make enough for one cake. *M. I. H.*

INSTANTANEOUS FROSTING.

To the white of an unbeaten egg add a c. and a quarter of pulverized sugar and stir until smooth. Add three drops of rose water, ten of vanilla and juice of half a lemon. It will at once become very white and harden in five or six m.

ORANGE FILLING FOR CAKE.

Carefully mix two tbsp. of flour in not more than two of cold milk. Pour over this half a pt. of milk that has just reached the boiling point. Stir constantly over the fire until it is thick and perfectly smooth; add the yolks of two eggs and four tbsp, sugar. Take from the fire; add the grated rind of one orange, and three tbsp. of orange juice. It should stand at least one h. in a cool place before putting between the layers.

Emma Belle Writt.

CHOCOLATE ICING.

Grate one cake German (or Maillard's) sweet chocolate. Add one lb. brown sugar, butter the size of an egg, one-half c milk, and boil all together gently, stirring to prevent burning. When the preparation has cooked until it is thick enough, flavor with vanilla, cool and spread between layers of the cake. If it should become too thick add two tbsp. milk and heat again to thoroughly mix.

SOFT GINGER CAKE.

Two c. New Orleans molasses, two-thirds c. butter, one even spoonful soda, one egg, three even c. sifted flour, one c. buttermilk, a pinch of salt. Mix molasses and butter and let come to a boil. When cool add a heaping tsp. brown ginger and the soda, then the other ingredients. Bake twenty m. in muffin pans.

Mrs. J. B. Washington.

SOFT GINGERBREAD.

Three c. sifted flour (six c. sifted flour), three eggs (six eggs), one c. of butter (one-half c. butter), one c. brown sugar (two c. brown sugar), one c. sugar house molasses (rather more than a pt. of molasses), one c. milk with tsp. soda in it, three tbsp. ginger (one-half c. ginger), one spoonful ground allspice. Mrs. Lee says

CAKE.

one c. sour cream instead of milk, with tbsp. of saleratus added after the other ingredients are thoroughly mixed.

Mrs. Price

SOFT GINGERBREAD.

Two lbs. flour, one lb. butter, one lb. brown sugar, two lbs. raisins stoned, ten eggs, one pt. molasses, one c. ginger, grated rind of two lemons, one tsp. soda dissolved in a c. of sour cream or buttermilk. Bake in bread pans.

" Cloud Capped."

SOFT GINGERBREAD.

One and one-half lb. of flour, one lb. of butter, one lb. nice brown sugar, one pt. molasses, eight eggs—beat separately—one c. of ground ginger, one tsp. of pearl ash dissolved in a tea c. of sour milk, one tsp. of allspice, one tsp. of mace, one tsp. of cinnamon, stoned plums and grated lemon peel (if you please) is an improvement.

Miss Sophia Campbell.

COOKIES.

Two c. sugar, one c. butter, three eggs, beaten separately, one-half a nutmeg, grated, one-half c. sour milk or cream, one-half tsp. soda, dissolved in cream, four c. flour, well sifted. Roll thin; sprinkle with granulated sugar and bake in a moderate oven.

Mrs. John H. Dalzell.

JUMBLES.

One lb. flour, one lb. white sugar, one lb. butter, four eggs, one nutmeg. Mix these ingredients well together; use extra flour for moulding, and use a spoon so as to handle them as little as possible. Bake in a moderate oven.

Mrs. H. L. Johnston.

CAKE.

SUGAR CAKES—"Best for Children."

One and one-half lb. flour, one lb. white sugar, one-half lb. butter, four eggs, one tea c. of sour cream, one tsp. of soda, one wineglass peach water. Cream the butter; rub in the flour very lightly. Use granulated sugar to roll them in instead of flour. They are better when made a few hours before baking; in winter, can be made the evening before. *Mrs. H. L. Johnston.*

SUGAR CAKES.

Five eggs, one lb. sugar, one-half lb. butter, as little flour as possible to mix pretty stiff, one wineglass of rose water (three tbsp.). *Miss Mary Johnston.*

TAYLOR CAKES.

One large c. butter, one c. brown sugar, three eggs, one pt. molasses, one-half pt. water, one tbsp. ginger, one tbsp. soda, two lbs. flour. Drop on greased pans.
Mrs. E. M. Ferguson.

SAND TARTS.

One lb. brown sugar, one-half lb. butter, three eggs, one-half c. sour milk, one tsp. of soda dissolved in the milk and added the last thing. Work butter and sugar together; add lightly beaten yolks of the egg, then one and one-quarter lb. of flour, good weight, and sift after weighing. Flour your board well and roll very thin. Cut in small shapes, any you may desire. Beat whites of eggs very light and wash over the cakes. Mix white sugar and cinnamon together and put on. Bake in an even oven.
Mrs. Wm. H. Singer, Jr.

CAKE. 151

DROP CAKES.

These cakes must be served fresh from the oven, sprinkled with powdered sugar. One c. pulverized sugar, one-half c. butter, two eggs, one-half c. milk, two tsp. vanilla, one and one-half c. flour, two tsp. baking powder sifted in the flour. Drop medium sized spoonfuls a little distance apart on buttered pans and bake in quick oven.

Mrs. Wm. R. Blair.

CREAM DROP CAKES.

Two c. sweet cream, two c. sugar, two eggs, one-half tsp. soda, enough flour to drop nicely. Flavor to taste.

Mrs. J. B. Washington.

COCOANUT DROP CAKES.

Cream well together one-half c. of butter and one c. of sugar, add the beaten yolks of two eggs, then alternately, one-third of a c. of milk and two c. of sifted flour. Beat well until smooth, add one scant tsp. of vanilla, one quarter of a tsp. of salt, one heaping c. of grated cocoanut, the stiffly whipped whites of the eggs and one heaping tsp. of baking powder. Beat for a moment and drop by the spoonful on well-greased pans. Flours vary so much that it may be necessary to add one or two spoonfuls more than the receipt calls for to keep them in shape. When baked and cold put away in a stone jar.

DROP GINGER CAKES.

One c. of lard and butter mixed, one c. Orleans molasses, three eggs well beaten together, one c. of sour milk, one c. of brown sugar, one tsp. of salt, one tbsp. of ginger, cloves and cinnamon, one large tbsp. of soda dissolved in boiling water and flour enough to make a stiff batter, drop on tins and bake. (Do not melt lard or butter.)

Mrs. Wilbert Frank.

DOUGHNUTS.

Dissolve one and one-half c. granulated sugar in one c. milk. To this add three well beaten eggs, four tbsp. of melted butter, one-half a nutmeg, and flour enough to roll out nicely. Be careful not to have it too stiff. About a qt. of flour to three tsp. of baking powder will do. Cut out and fry in *boiling* lard. The lard must more than cover them when raised. Sprinkle with pulvarized sugar mixed with nutmeg. Mixing the sugar with the milk prevents the dough from soaking grease and avoids the use of a great deal of flour in working with the dough. It makes the cakes puffy and delicate.

Mrs. Alexander B. Sheppard.

NUT CAKES.

One lb. sugar, one lb. nuts, whites of six eggs. Beat sugar and eggs together until light; then add nuts. Drop on greased pans. Bake in a moderate oven.

Mrs. Chauncey F. Black.

HICKORY NUT MACAROONS.

White of one egg well beaten, add one c. sugar and beat thoroughly, one c. nut meats chopped fine; make into balls size of large hickorynut; roll in flour and drop on buttered pans, and bake in moderate oven.

Dillie Hays.

154 CAKE.

CAKE.

BEVERAGES.

COFFEE.

Mix coffee in the proportion of one-third Java, one-third Mocha, one-third Laguyra. *Gilmore Hoffman.*

FRENCH COFFEE.

Two parts Mocha coffee carefully roasted and ground, one part best Government Java, roasted and ground. To every three tbsp. of ground coffee, one tsp. of chicory, and make the coffee as usual. Then when you put the milk on to boil put in a *large* pinch of pearl barley and strain the milk after it is boiled.

Mrs. Burns (on board Scotia.)

BOILED COFFEE.

One heaping tbsp. coffee to one c. boiling water. Measure the ground coffee, moisten it with a little cold water and add the shell of an egg and a *little* of the white. Too much white of egg weakens the coffee. Put the mixture into a *heated* coffee pot and pour on the freshly boiled water. Boil for five m., add one-fourth c. cold water and remove to a cooler part of the range. After standing a few m. it is ready to serve. Coffee is improved by re-heating just before serving.

BEVERAGES.

FILTERED COFFEE.

One heaping tbsp. coffee to one c. boiling water. The coffee, finely ground, is put into the upper part of a French coffee-pot which has been heated and the boiling water poured through it. The coffee-pot must be kept in a warm place while the coffee is being made.

TEA.

One tsp. tea to one c. freshly boiled water. Heat the teapot; place tea in teapot; pour freshly boiled water over it, and steep a few m.

ICED TEA.

One large pot of Heno Tea, very strong. Sweeten to taste, and add the juice of six lemons, with plenty of crushed ice. Put a few slices of lemon in the pitcher when ready to serve. *Jane.*

CHOCOLATE.

To every half lb. of Maillard's double vanilla chocolate use one and one-half c. of hot water and three c. of milk. Break the chocolate into small pieces, put it in saucepan and pour over it the hot water. Set it on the back of range to dissolve. When ready to serve add the milk and stir constantly until it boils and thickens.

Each half lb. cake is divided into six cakes and will make six c. of chocolate. *Mrs. Byron H. Painter.*

CHOCOLATE.

To each paper Maillard's chocolate (broken into small pieces) add one and one-half coffee c. water. Let stand to soften and dissolve, then add three coffee c. of milk, put on the fire and allow to boil for ten m. stirring every now and then. *Mrs. John W. Chalfant.*

BEVERAGES.

TO PREPARE CHOCOLATE.

Each one-half lb. is divided into six pieces. Each piece is the quantity for one c. Take a tin pan and pour in one-half a glass of warm water; break the chocolate in small pieces and let it dissolve in the water, stirring constantly. When dissolved mix with a c. of warm milk and stir again over the fire until it boils three or four m. Then the chocolate is done and perfect. It is very necessary that it should *boil* to be good.   *Henry Maillard.*

INDIAN LEMONADE.

Pare two oranges and two lemons as thin as possible, and steep them for four h. in one qt. hot water. Boil one and one-fourth lb. loaf sugar in three pts. of water. Skim it, and add to the two liquors the juice of six oranges and twelve lemons. Strain through a jelly bag and serve ice cold.   *Mrs. J. B. Washington.*

PUNCH.

One-half tumbler Jamaica rum, one-half tumbler brandy, one tumbler sugar, three tumblers water, one lemon. To be well iced.   *Mr. Travers.*

PHILADELPHIA FISH HOUSE PUNCH.

One pt. brandy, two pts. rum, and a wineglass peach brandy. To the three pts. of liquor add nine pts. water, one pt. lemon juice, and two lbs. white sugar. Ice well before using. One lb. ice is equal to one pt. of water. Enough for twenty-five persons.   *Mrs. Peters.*

THE MANSION HOUSE LOVING CUP—Sent Me By the Lady Mayoress.

Take one bottle Port wine, one bottle Claret, one bottle Madeira, two wineglasses of Curacao. Put all into a jug ; then one oz. of cloves, one oz. of cinnamon, one-half oz. of nutmeg, ground together, boiled in a pt. of water for a quarter of an h. ; then strain the water through a fine linen cloth and mix all together. Bottle the same and ice it. *Mrs. H. L. Johnston.*

TEA PUNCH.

One qt. sherry wine, one and one-fourth lb. cut sugar, six lemons, one c. green tea (Gunpowder tea) as strong as lye. Peel the lemons and pour the hot tea over the rinds. Pour the lemon juice over the sugar. After the tea is cold strain it from the rind and pour over the lemon and sugar, add the wine, strain again and pour over fine crushed ice. *Mrs. Keyser.*

APPLE TODDY.

Six apples, one-half pt. rum, one qt. whiskey and boiling water and sugar added to taste.
Mrs. Carroll Winchester.

APPLE TOD.

One red streaked apple roasted on a china plate before a slow fire. Put it into a tumbler, mash well and add one glass good brandy. Let stand twelve hours then add two wineglasses of water, a little nutmeg and a spoonful of sugar. *Mrs. Perine.*

EGG NOGG.

To every egg a wineglass of brandy a tbsp. of granulated sugar and a tumbler of cream (these are the proper proportions). To every twelve yolks, three whites, beat up very light separately, mix them together and beat again as if for a pudding ; then add the sugar and

BEVERAGES. 161

beat again ; then add the brandy gradually, stirring all the time ; then stir in by degrees the cream. Flavor, if you choose, with a little rum and peach brandy.

Mrs. Owings Hoffman.

EGG NOGG.

Five qts. of cream, eight tumblers of brandy, sixty eggs, five lb. white sugar. Beat the yolks and sugar together, add the brandy by degrees, and lastly the cream. *Mrs. Joseph White.*

EGG NOGG.

Fourteen wineglasses brandy, seven of Jamaica spirits, mix and set aside. Beat the yolks of twenty eggs with twenty tbsp. sugar, and pour in gradually the mixed liquors. Beat the whites with two tbsp. sugar very light and mix half of this into the yolks and liquor. Pour in slowly two qts. cream and put the other whites of the eggs on top. *Maryland Club.*

EGG NOGG.

One pt. brandy, one-half pt. old rum, two qts. cream, one doz. eggs and one lb. powdered loaf sugar.

Mrs. Carroll Winchester.

HOCK CUP.

Place three pieces of loaf sugar, a few torn leaves of fresh mint and the juice and thinly pared rind of a lemon in a two qt. glass pitcher. Fill the pitcher to the top with finely crushed ice and pour over the whole one qt. white wine. Stir well, place a bunch of mint in the top of the pitcher and allow to stand for a few m. before serving. *Major Burbank.*

BEVERAGES.

MULLED WINE.

Into a saucepan put one tbsp. of white cloves, one tsp. of whole allspice, a two-inch stick of cinnamon and one pt. of boiling water. Cover closely and simmer until reduced one-half. Strain, add one-half of a c. of sugar and one pt. of claret, reheat almost to the boiling point and serve.

MULLED WINE

One qt. of Sherry or Madeira wine, half a tea c. of whole allspice (tied up in a net bag). Put *half* the wine and all of the water and allspice on to boil. Beat the yellows of seven eggs with a lb. of sugar and the remaining wine. When the *water, wine and allspice* has boiled for *five* m., pour it over the sugar, etc., and beat hard. Pour all back into the kettle and let it *nearly* boil again, stirring constantly. Have the whites beaten to a stiff froth, and pour all together into your punch bowl or pitcher, and add a large tumblerful of cream, and the same of brandy. Serve at once.

Mrs. A. E. W. Painter.

FROM LONG'S HOTEL, LONDON.
Cider Cup.

One bottle of cider (one qt.), one bottle seltzer, one and one-half liqueur glasses of brandy, one-half liqueur glass of curacao, four drops of Maraschino, ice, two slices of lemon, burridge or cucumber peel, one dessert spoon of castor sugar.

Put ice first always; then burridge and lemon; then liqueurs and sugar; then the cider, and last seltzer.

BEVERAGES.

Hock Cup.

Substitute hock for cider and use two dessert spoons of sugar.

Claret Cup.

Same as hock cup—use claret instead of hock.

Champagne Cup.

One bottle of champagne, one liqueur glass of brandy, one liqueur glass of curacao, one-fourth liqueur glass of Maraschino, one bottle of seltzer, ice, burridge or cucumber peel, two slices of lemon peel.

Mr. Douglas Stewart.

CIDER CUP.

One qt. cider, one-third tumbler brandy, one-third tumbler sherry, one qt. Apollionaris, one can of pineapple. Add syrup and loaf sugar if not sweet enough. Sliced oranges and lemons to suit the taste

Mrs. Horace G. Dravo.

MINT JULEP.

Place a piece of sugar and a few torn leaves of mint in a tall glass and add one tbsp. water, or barely enough to dissolve the sugar. Then fill the glass to the top, packing it tight, with fine crushed ice. Last, pour in as much whisky as the ice will allow and stir in the center for several m. with a *silver fork*. This will cause a thick frost to form on the outside of the glass.

Mrs. A. P. Burgwin.

CHERRY CORDIAL.

Stone the best of cherries (May Dukes or English Morellos) and let them remain over night in the refrigerator. Next morning strain, and to every qt. of juice allow two lbs. of coarse granulated sugar and a qt. of good California brandy. Add the sugar to the juice and stir until thoroughly dissolved, then add the brandy and strain again. Bottle and seal up.

Mrs. Byron H. Painter.

BLACKBERRY WINE.

To every gal. of berries previously mashed, add one qt. soft water. After a thorough fermentation dip off the clear juice and press seeds, etc. To every gal. juice add two and one-half lbs. white coffee sugar, put into barrels, cover bung holes with coarse wire gauze and after the second fermentation has taken place draw off and filter through flannel or gauze. Place in barrels and put in the bungs. The oftener it is filtered the purer and better it will be. In making large quantities a cider press would be very useful.

Mrs. J. B. Washington.

GINGER BEER.

Two lbs. loaf sugar, one and one-half oz. ginger—bruised, three lemons, juice and peel, two gals. boiling water poured over it. When luke warm add two tbsp. yeast with the whites of two eggs well whipped. Cover with a heavy blanket. The next day skim and bottle.

Mrs. J. B. Washington.

BEVERAGES. 167

PRESERVES AND PICKLES.

QUINCE JELLY.

Wash and wipe the quinces, cut them in pieces, using cores and all. Cover them with water, and boil until very soft. Mash and strain them. To every pt. of juice, put a lb. of sugar, and let it boil till it forms a jelly, say one-half an h., but always try by cooling in a spoon until it leaves the spoon in a mass. If you wish to preserve the quinces or put them in pear butter, the cores and skins make good jelly. *Mrs. I. Hager.*

CURRANT JELLY.

Put currants, stems and all, into a crock ; pound them with a potato masher, and then strain them through a bag. Put two or four pts. of juice in a kettle, and let it boil twenty m. (the less juice that is put on at a time the more delicate the jelly). Stir in two or four lbs. of sugar (one lb. to one pt.) *just long* enough to dissolve it, and pour into cups. If left a m. *too long* on the fire the jelly will be thick *like custard.* *Mrs. I. Hager.*

CONSERVES.

To six lbs. of *ripe* fruit allow two lbs. of sugar, one qt. of water. Put all in a kettle together ; boil until perfectly soft, then take out the fruit, spread on dishes and sun for two days. Then put the fruit again in the kettle with the same syrup and let boil. Spread again on dishes and expose to the sun and air till perfectly dry and pack away in sugar. The fruit should be turned frequently (and the dishes changed) while drying.

Miss Emily Upshur Johnston.

TO PRESERVE STRAWBERRIES.

Weigh the strawberries and take their weight in sugar; put them into the kettle together, no water, or not more than a wineglass full, and let them boil up well. Pour them into a bowl and let them stand until the next day. Give them another boil, and perhaps that will do. If not clear boil them a third time. *Mrs. Johnston.*

PEAR BUTTER.

Our kettle holds a little more than one and one-half bushels. A little over one bushel pears and less than one-half bushel of quinces (the right proportion for a large kettle is one-half bushel quinces to two and one-half bushel pears), twenty lbs. sugar, one oz. ground cinnamon, one-half oz. ground cloves. *Mrs. Schroeder.*

ORANGE MARMALADE.

Cover one doz. seedless oranges with water and boil until skin is soft enough to easily insert the head of a pin. When cool, thinly slice the peel and shred the pulp in small pieces. To every lb. of fruit add two lbs. granulated sugar, one-half pt. water in which oranges were boiled and the juice of three large or four small lemons.

PRESERVES AND PICKLES. 171

Boil this mixture for about an h., or until thick. This quantity of fruit makes about eight full pts. of marmalade. *Mrs. John Hampton.*

GINGER PEARS.

Eight lbs. of pears cut in small cubes, eight lbs. of sugar, one lb. of green ginger root, four lemons cut in small pieces. Cook pears, sugar and ginger together slowly with very little water, when partly done add lemons and cook until clear and tender, let simmer until brown. *Mrs. John W. Chalfant.*

SPICED CURRANTS.

Five lbs. currants, weighed after being stemmed, four and one-half lbs. white sugar, two lemons, rind and all chopped fine, one tbsp. cloves, two tbsp. cinnamon, one c. vinegar. Boil slowly two h. until the consistency of apple butter. *Mrs. J. B. Washington.*

BRANDIED PEACHES.

Pare your peaches and then weigh them, taking half their weight in sugar. Make syrup in the proportion of four lbs. of granulated sugar to one pt. of water. Boil the syrup and skim until perfectly clear. Place the peaches in the syrup and allow them to cook until they crack open on the sides, then take them out and allow the syrup to cook until it becomes quite thick. When cold add one pt. of brandy or rum to one pt. of syrup. Mix well and pour over your peaches which have been placed in glass jars. *Mrs. H. P. Allen.*

BRANDIED PEACHES

To every lb. of pared peaches allow three-fourths lb. of sugar. Make a rich syrup, put in the peaches and cook until tender. Take them out and drop them in the brandy. Boil the syrup until thick and use half brandy and half syrup to pour over your peaches.

Miss Donaldson.

CUCUMBER PICKLE.

Six doz. cucumbers, one lb. mustard, one-fourth pk. onions, one lb. mustard seed, six red peppers, one tbsp. celery seed, six sticks horseradish, two lbs. brown sugar, three qts. and one pt. vinegar.

Pare and slice the cucumbers and salt them, allowing them to remain in the salt over night. Next morning drain dry and add the cut up pepper and horseradish, and mix in the mustard seed and celery seed. Put two qts. and one pt. of the vinegar on in the kettle, and when it is boiling, add the sugar and then the mustard, which has been well mixed with the other qt. of vinegar. Cook this until very thick, and then add all the other ingredients, and cook until all is very thick. Excellent pickle.

Mrs. Albert H. Childs.

GREEN TOMATO PICKLE.

Slice one-half bushel green tomatoes, twenty-four large onions, sprinkle with salt, and let drain in basket all night. Squeeze out, put into a kettle, cover with vinegar, and boil twenty m. Let stand in this vinegar till next day. Squeeze out, put into a kettle, cover with fresh vinegar, and add two lbs. sugar, one-half lb. white mustard seed, one-fourth lb. black mustard seed, one small box mustard, seventeen cloves, one oz. each of allspice, mace, white pepper corns, celery seed and two oz. tumeric. Boil until just a little tender. When cold, add one pt. olive oil, one c. mustard sauce.

Mrs. J. B. Washington.

PRESERVES AND PICKLES.

WALNUT PICKLES.

Walnuts (English) for pickling must be gathered before the 20th of June, when you can stick a pin through them, put them in strong salt and water until they turn black, Boil good cider vinegar with spices and pepper and throw the walnuts in the boiling vinegar. Not good for a year after made. *Mrs. Nicholson.*

MARTINA PICKLES.

Put tender martinas in a strong brine for one week. Take them out, drain them, and put in cold vinegar leaving them for two weeks. To one gal. vinegar put three lbs. brown sugar, one-half a c. of allspice, one-half c. of pounded cloves and one-half c. of black pepper, two tbsp. of celery seed, three pods of red pepper. Pound them all together, boil them in the vinegar, and pour it over the martinas. Scraped horseradish is an improvement, if added. *Mrs. Brichhead.*

MANGOE PICKLES.

Take a doz. small green mangoes, cut them in half, remove the seeds, and cover with brine strong enough to bear an egg. Leave them in the brine for one week, then pare them thinly and put over a slow fire in a kettle of water lined with grape leaves. Simmer until they are moderately soft, then take from the fire and when cool fill with the following preparation :

Filling for One Dozen Mangoes.

One lb. white mustard seed, washed and swelled, two pts. horse radish, one bottle salad oil, one pt. brown sugar, one-half c. celery seed, a few small onions chopped, a little mace, nutmeg, cinnanon and cloves. When this

PRESERVES AND PICKLES.

is all mixed thoroughly, use it to stuff the mangoes. Place them in a stone jar and pour over them boiling vinegar in which some brown sugar has been dissolved. Tie up closely and put away. These pickles are not good until a year after making. "*Friendship Hill.*"

SWEET PICKLE.

Seven lbs. cucumbers, one qt. vinegar, two and one-half lbs. sugar, one and one-half oz. each of mace, cinnamon, cloves and ginger. Scald with boiling vinegar three times. Prepare medium sized cucumbers, soak in strong brine one week and scald them three mornings with one-half vinegar and half water, alum the size of a cherry. Cut the cucumbers in quarters. *Mrs. Cooper.*

WATERMELON PICKLE.

Take the rind of one good sized melon and put in salt water over night. Then pare off the green outer rind and the pink soft part and cut in small squares or strips. Stick a few cloves in each piece and cook in the following mixture, after it has come to the boiling point, for half an h. or forty-five m. : One qt. best cider vinegar, three qts. brown sugar, a little mace, stick cinnamon, cloves, white ginger root and allspice. It is an improvement to add two sliced lemons when the melon rind is put into the syrup. *Mary C. Speer.*

SWEET PICKLED CANTALOUPE

Take a fine large cantaloupe, not quite ripe enough to eat ; pare and cut in slices about an inch thick. Just cover with vinegar for twenty-four h., then pour off and measure the vinegar, leaving out one qt. To what remains add three lbs. brown sugar to each qt. and cinna-

PRESERVES AND PICKLES. 175

mon, cloves and mace to taste. Put on the fire in a kettle and when it boils add the melon. Cook about one-half an h. until it looks clear. It will be ready for use in two or three weeks. *Mrs. Keyser.*

PICKLED OYSTERS.

One qt. oysters, one tbsp. salt, put into a. preserving kettle and boil about ten m., until the gills turn up. Skim them well. Take out the oysters, put into a colander and run cold water on them for fifteen m. Add to the liquor one-half as much vinegar as there is liquor, a few cloves, allspice, white peppercorns, a blade of mace; boil and pour over oysters. *Mrs. Keyser.*

TOMATO CATSUP.

Select ripe tomatoes and mash with the hands to extract all the juice. Let all come to a boil and then strain through a sieve. To every two gals. of juice add six tbsp. salt, three even tbsp. black pepper, four even tbsp. mustard, one tbsp. each of cayenne pepper, ground allspice and ground cloves, the latter two in a bag, one qt. strong cider vinegar, one lb. brown sugar. Boil down until thick and smooth. *Mrs. J. B. Washington.*

CHILI SAUCE.

Four doz. ripe tomatoes, ten green peppers and twelve white onions chopped fine. Add eight tbsp. salt, twelve tbsp. brown sugar and four c. strong cider vinegar. Boil three h. and add just before taking off one-half oz. celery seed. *Mrs. J. W. Washington.*

TOMATO SAUCE.

Slice, sprinkle and let drain in a basket all night one pk. tomatoes and twelve large onions. Then add one lb. sugar, one-quarter lb. white mustard seed, one small box mustard, one oz. each of mace, cloves and pepper, two oz. celery seed. Cover all with strong vinegar and cook until tender. *Mrs. McKenzie.*

PRESERVES AND PICKLES.

CANDY.

CHOCOLATE CARAMELS.

One lb. brown sugar, one-fourth lb. chocolate (four oz.), one-half c. cream, one-half c. butter, one-half c. molasses, one tbsp. vanilla, one c. chopped nuts. Cook all together except the vanilla and the nuts. When the temperature is 254° Fahr., remove from the range, add vanilla and nuts and pour into shallow pans which have been well buttered. If too soft add a little milk and cook again to same temperature. This may be done several times if there is trouble getting them hard.

CHOCOLATE CARAMELS.

Two c. brown sugar, one c. molasses, one-half c. milk, piece of butter the size of an egg. To this quantity use one package Maillard's or German sweet chocolate and one tbsp. vanilla. Boil about half an h.

CHOCOLATE CARAMELS.

One-half lb. Baker's chocolate, one c. rich milk or cream, one-fourth lb. butter, one and one-half lb. sugar, one-half tbsp. vanilla. The only way to tell when the caramels are done is by placing a little of the candy on a saucer and stirring with a fork—when it creams and becomes firm it must be taken from the stove *immediately* and poured onto a large well buttered meat platter and stirred vigorously with a fork until it thickens and becomes firm. Cut in squares before it is cold.

Mrs. J. L Dawson Speer.

TAFFY.

One qt. Orleans molasses, one c. white sugar, one tbsp. butter, one tbsp. vinegar. Boil all together and try in water to see when it is done. Just before taking from the stove add a small one-half tsp. soda.

WHITE TAFFY.

Two lbs. white sugar, enough water to melt it, one tbsp. butter, one tbsp. vinegar, one tbsp. vanilla, one tsp. cream tartar ; put all in at once except vanilla. Do not stir while boiling. *Emma F. Peterson.*

EVERTON TAFFY.

One lb. of white sugar, one c. of cold water, one oz. of butter; add one tbsp. of vinegar; when it boils twenty m., add one dessert spoonful of vanilla and pour in buttered plates. " *Cloud Capped.*"

ALMOND CANDY

One lb. maple sugar, one pt. cream. When the preparation comes to a boil add one lb. blanched almonds.

Miss J. McC. Taylor.

PEANUT CANDY.

One c. granulated sugar, one c. rolled peanuts. The nuts are prepared by chopping, by rolling with a wooden pin or by putting through the meat chopper. Warm the

CANDY. 183

sugar in a pan in the oven. Put it into a heated French pan. When it has melted remove to the back of the range and add the peanuts, mixing them thoroughly with the melted sugar. Spread in a tin and press into shape with knives. The tin does not need greasing. Cut into bars. The candy hardens immediately.

TOFFEE.

One lb. brown sugar, one-half c. butter, one lemon or four tbsp. vinegar, English walnuts. Heat the sugar, butter and acid over moderate heat. When the mixture bubbles, stop stirring, and cook to 270° Fahr. Pour it over the nuts, which have been put on well buttered pans. It hardens in a few minutes.

COCOANUT BAR.

Four c. sugar, one c. water, one-half tsp cream of tartar, one-fourth lb. cocoanut. Stir the sugar, water and cream of tartar together until the sugar is dissolved. As soon as the mixture bubbles, cook without stirring until it reaches 238° Fahr. Remove immediately from the range. Cool (but not in a very cold place); then beat until it thickens, and add the cocoanut. Desiccated cocoanut may be used. Spread on buttered pans. Cool, but not in cold place, as cold hardens the top. It should be soft and creamy. Cut into bars.

MARSHMALLOWS.

Dissolve a half lb. of gum arabic in one pt. of water; strain and add half a lb. of white sugar. Place over the fire, stirring constantly until the syrup is dissolved and cooked to the consistency of honey; take from the fire, add gradually to the whites of four eggs well beaten; stir the mixture until it is somewhat thin, and does not adhere to the fingers. Flavor to taste; pour into a tin slightly dusted with powdered starch; put in a warm place, and when firm enough cut in small squares.

MISCELLANEOUS.

RECEIPT FOR MAKING COLOGNE.

Oil of bergamot, two drachms; oil of lemon, one drachm; oil of neroli, twenty drops ; oil of origanum, six drops ; oil of rosemary, twenty drops ; alcohol, triple distilled, one pt. ; orange-flower water, one oz.
Mrs. H. B. Wilkins.

FOR CHAPPED HANDS.

Six oz. of witch-hazel, one oz. of bay-rum, one-half oz. spirits of camphor, one-half oz. of glycerine.
From " The Country Gentleman."

POT-POURRI.—Old Fashioned June Roses.

Gather the roses quite dry, pull them from their stalks, leaving out all wet or decayed leaves; put with them a small quantity of lavender and orange flowers. Lay them in a glazed jar in thick layers, strew freely with bag salt between each layer, pressing them down with the hand. Put away with a cover on, and let remain two weeks. At the end of that time pour off any liquor and press the leaves with the hands, break in pieces, getting all moisture out. Then prepare the following mixture: one ounce each cloves, mace, cinnamon, gum benzoine, orris root, sliced sandalwood, a small quantity of *musk*. Mix all this with the rose leaves, put in a jar, stirring frequently. *Mrs. Horace G. Dravo.*

TO STEAM VELVET

Steam velvet by wetting thoroughly on the wrong side and pass the wrong side over a very hot iron quickly.

TO REMOVE MILDEW—No. 1.

One-fourth lb. chloride of lime in two gals. of water. Let it stand one h. and pour off and strain. Put the clothes in and let them stand two h., then wash well. (This I like best, and have used frequently; No. 2 I keep for *stains*.) *Mrs. I. Hager.*

TO TAKE OUT MILDEW—No. 2.

Take one-half lb. chloride of lime, powder it and put on it two qts. cold water. Stir it well and then let it settle. Pour off the liquid and strain and bottle it, cork tightly. Cover the stains or mildew with the liquid. It can remain on several days without injury, and may then be washed out. *Mrs. I. Hager.*

BENZINE CLEANING FLUID.

One drachm sulphuric ether, one drachm chloroform, two drachms alcohol mixed with one drachm oil of wintergreen, one qt. deodorized benzine.

Mrs. Byron H. Painter.

CLEANING COMPOUND.

One-half oz. alcohol, one-fourth oz. white castile soap, one-half oz. sulphuric ether, one-fourth lb. aqua

MISCELLANEOUS.

ammonia, one-half oz. glycerine. Dissolve soap in one pt. soft water, then add two qts. more water and the other ingredients and bottle for use.

Mrs. McKennan.

CLEANING FLUID.

Will remove all grease spots from clothes. Three oz. Williams' shaving soap, two oz. ammonia, one oz. saltpetre and enough water to make one gal. in all.

L. W. Washington.

TO CLEAN CARPETS AND WOOLENS.

Four oz. aqua ammonia, one oz. sulphuric ether, one oz. glycerine, one oz. alcohol, and four oz. Castile soap. Shave the soap. Pour over it one qt. tepid water. Keep on the fire until dissolved, then add three qts. tepid water. When this cools, add the other ingredients, and bottle, *corking tightly*. Rub on with a sponge, and wipe with a clean cloth.

For carpets, mix with a little more water; scrub, and rub with a dry cloth. *Mrs. J. B. Washington.*

ENGLISH RECIPE FOR CLEANING WALL PAPER.

Sufficient flour to make three loaves of bread. One-half wheat flour and one-half rye flour; one tbsp. salt, two tbsp. pulverized alum, some washing blue, one cake yeast. Raise as for bread, and bake one h. While warm, cut off the crust and put into a large bowl and pour over it one c. water. Knead into a stiff dough, like putty. Squeeze into balls and rub paper in one direction. *Mrs. J. B. Washington.*

MISCELLANEOUS.

TO MAKE LYE.

Fill your lye hopper with good ashes, four weeks before you make your soap. Throw into it a bucket or two of water, every two or three days, and when you make your lye pour in boiling water until you make it strong enough to bear an egg.

TO MAKE HARD SOAP.

To clarify the fat put the grease into a kettle of cold water; after it has boiled run it through a coarse cloth and set aside to cool. The fat will settle in a cake. Put into a pot that will hold twelve gals., twelve lbs. of fat (always a lb. of fat to a gal. of water), and let it get boiling hot; add to it two gals. *strong* lye. When it again becomes boiling hot put in two gals. more. After that let it boil as quickly as possible, stirring it all the time, and feeding it with lye as it begins to boil over, until the pot is nearly full. When there is no more grease, and it seems well incorporated, the soap is done. Then stir into the twelve gals. about three pts. salt until it mixes well, it will take about a quarter of an h.

TO MAKE SOFT SOAP

Allow sixteen lbs. grease and sixteen lbs. potash for a barrel of soap. The grease should be good, neither mouldy nor wormy. The potash should be the color of pumice stone. That which is red makes dark soap. Cut grease into pieces of about one or two oz. and put it into a tight barrel with the potash. Then pour in two pailfuls of rain or spring water. The soap will be soonest made by heating the water, but it is just as sure to be good if made with cold water. Add one-half pailful of

MISCELLANEOUS.

water every day until the barrel is one-half full, stirring it well each day. A long stick with a cross-piece at the lower end is the best for this purpose When the barrel is one-half full, add no more water for a week or ten days, but continue to stir daily; after that continue to add a pailful every day until the barrel is full. It is best to keep soap three or four months before using. Soft soap made of clear grease and good potash is of a light nankeen color and is better for washing flannels and white clothes than any other.

TO RENDER MUTTON SUET.

Take the *kidney-fat* of suet, cut it in small pieces, and put it into a saucepan, with about one tbsp. water to keep it from burning. When the fat separates from the cracklings, strain it into a dish with one-half c. milk. Let it stand until the next day, then take it off the milk and put it again into the saucepan, with a little more milk. When it melts pour in a few drops of rose water, and pour it into cups. When cold take it out of the cups and the dregs will be found at the bottom with the milk.

TO TAKE STAINS OUT OF WHITE CLOTHES.

First apply chloride of soda and if that does not remove the stain use oxalic acid dissolved in water.

TO TAKE OUT INK.

A mixture of soft soap, tallow, salt and lemon juice. First wash out the ink in water, and then, when the mixture is hot, lay the ink spot in it.

TO CLEAN WHITE PAINT.

Use powdered French chalk and hot water. French chalk is the common steatite or soap stone. Use *no* soap.

MISCELLANEOUS.

TO SET THE COLORS OF CALICOES.

A weak solution of alum water will set the colors in printed goods of all descriptions.

Calicoes should be washed in three fresh lathers of the best soap, and then in three or four rinsing waters.

To set the colors of green, yellow, fawn, maroon, drab and stone, throw a handful of salt in the last water.

To set the color of lilac and purple use *strong* alum water in the last rinsing water.

Use soft water whenever possible for washing calicoes and prepare the lather by boiling the soap in the water. Wash the goods when the lather is milk warm. It is best to have two lathers prepared at once so as to wash the material as quickly as possible. *Always* dry in the *shade*. The day must be a clear one.

TO WASH FLANNEL.

This must be done on a *clear* day and when washed must be put out as quickly as possible to dry. Wash in a strong lather of soap and water, as hot as your hands can bear. Carry through two or three waters if necessary and let the last water be a light lather of soap instead of clear water, as that will keep the flannel white. As soon as it is washed shake it out and hang in the wind and sun to dry as quickly as possible. When nearly dry, just to feel a dampness in it, shake, stretch and fold it smooth. Put it in a press and let it stay all night, or until sufficiently pressed. Take it out and iron out the strings and bindings, *but not* the flannel, as that would turn it yellow.

MISCELLANEOUS.

TO WASH BLACK LACE OR NET.

Half a pt. of spirits of wine, and one tbsp. gum arabic. Dip it in this mixture. When nearly dry, iron it carefully.

TO TAKE SPOTS OUT OF MATTING.

For a yellow spot or stain on matting, wash with a weak solution of oxalic acid (six cents' worth in one gal. water). If too strong, it will turn it white.

To restore a white spot to the original color, use a weak solution of carbonate of soda.

TO TAKE INK OUT OF CARPETS.

Cover the spot at once with raw potato scraped to a pulp, and renew as often as the paste becomes discolored.

TO TAKE GREASE OUT OF CARPETS.

Cover the spot with buckwheat batter prepared for baking.

TO TAKE SPOTS OUT OF MARBLE HEARTHS.

Pearl ash, fuller's earth and whiting mixed with spirits of wine to a paste, and put on the spots. Wash off every morning with soap and water, and renew until the spots disappear.

TO CLEAN WHITE MARBLE HEARTHS.

Rub the marble with *grit* first and pumice stone afterward.

TO DRIVE AWAY ANTS.

The little red ants will leave closets where sea sand is sprinkled, or where oyster shells are laid.

Scatter sprigs of wormwood where black ants are troublesome.

MISCELLANEOUS.

TO KEEP EGGS UNTIL WINTER.

Place a layer of sawdust or salt in a keg. Pack the eggs closely with the small ends down. Over this another layer of salt or saw dust; packing closely between the eggs, where they must not touch; and so on alternately, until the keg is full. Head it up tightly and turn it from end to end every twenty-four h.

MARKING WITH INDELIBLE INK.

If you wash the spot on the articles to be marked, with a mixture of as much saleratus as a qt. of water will take up, and a lump of gum-arabic, you will find that the marking will be much easier and will look much better.

TO CLEAN PRINTS AND ENGRAVINGS.

Wash them with chlorine of different degrees of strength, according to the stain. Chlorine will generally remove the stain, and have no effect upon the ink used in printing. *Mrs. J. B. Washington.*

KEEPING FURNITURE BRIGHT.

Wash thoroughly with warm soapy water, drying as quickly as possible; then with a flannel rag dipped in a mixture of two parts linseed to one of kerosene, rub the surface thoroughly. Let it stand until you have rubbed another piece, and then with a perfectly clean piece of flannel free from oil, polish until it shines to your taste. It will not hurt the daintiest wood and the odor soon evaporates. If there is much furniture to be polished mix a little at a time. Clean oil and clean rags make much better results. *Mrs. J. B. Washington.*

MISCELLANEOUS.

TO KEEP FLOWERS FRESH.

Put a small quantity of alum in the water in which they are placed. This is best done by dissolving alum in hot water and adding to fresh water in the proportion of about one tbsp. to one pt.

TO PREVENT MOULD ON PRESERVES.

Mould can be kept off the top of preserves by putting a few drops of glycerine around the edges of the jar before screwing on the cover.

TO TAKE COVERS OFF FRUIT JARS.

If the fruit jar covers are difficult to remove, invert the jar and place it in hot water for a m. or two. You will be surprised to find how easily the cover yields to a very slight effort.

SILVER POLISH.

One lb. Gilder's whiting, three oz. alcohol, one-fourth pt. ammonia, one pt. water.

Mrs. J. B. Washington.

TO REMOVE RUST FROM KNIVES OR ANY STEEL.

Cover with sweet oil, then with dry lime on a woolen rag, rub them well, afterwards with dry pearl ash in the same way. Oil them again and put them aside. Repeat the process, if necessary, for two or three days and the rust will entirely disappear.

To finish off and make them bright mix oil and rotten stone and polish them well.

MISCELLANEOUS.

TO CLEAN BRASS.

Clean brass (lamps, fenders, etc.) with rotten stone; mix oxalic acid very weak with water and use just enough of the mixture to moisten the rotten stone.

TO CLEAN TINS.

Clean tins with brick dust and lard and they will be beautiful.

TO TAKE SPOTS OFF GILT.

To take spots off of gilt.—White of egg applied with a camel's hair brush. *Mrs. H. L. Johnston.*

MISCELLANEOUS.

INDEX.

SOUPS.
Beef Tea 3
Calf's Head Soup 2
Chestnut Soup 4
Chicken Curry, with Rice . . 3
Clam Soup . . . 1
Clear Soup 1
Corn Soup 4
Green Corn and Tomato Soup 5
Green Pea Soup 6
Marrow Balls 6
Mutton Broth . . . 4
Okra Soup 1
Ox Tail Soup 2
Rice Soup 5
Rice and Tomato Soup 5
Turkey Soup 3

FISH.
Crabs, Soft 12
Fish à la Creme 15
Fish Balls 15
Halibut à la Creme 14
Little Pigs in Blankets 12
Lobster à la Newburg . . . 13
Oysters à la Newburg . . . 11
Oysters Fricassee 11
Oysters on Chafing Dish . . . 11
Oysters Panned 12
Rock Fish à la Creme 14
Salmon with Sauce, Dressed . . 15
Shad Cutlets 13
Shad Roe 13

ROLLS, MUFFINS, ETC.
Baking Powder Biscuit 25
Biscuit, Sherwood 24
Boston Brown Bread 21
Bread Cake 27
Brown Flour Muffins 23
Buckwheat Cakes 28
Buttermilk Cakes 27
Corn Bread 24
Corn Cakes 28
Corn Fritters 28
Corn Fritters 28
Corn Muffins 25
Delicious Corn Bread 25
Drop Biscuit 25
Egg Pone 24
English Muffins 24
Fritters 30
German Pancakes 29
German Toast 31
Graham Griddle Cakes . . . 30
Grits Muffins 23
" Hermitage " Muffins 23
Maryland Biscuit 26
Milk Toast 31
Pop Overs 27
Potato Rolls 21
Potato Rolls 22
Rice Cakes 29
Rice Cakes 29
Rolls 21
Rusk 22
Rusk 23

INDEX.

Sally Lunn 31
Short Bread, Margaret's Scotch . 26
Soda Crackers 26
Turn Overs . . . 22
Wafers 26
Waffles 30
Waffles, Rice . . 31
Waffles, Risen 30

EGGS AND CHEESE.

Baked Eggs 37
Baked Eggs 38
Cheese Fondue 39
Cheese Pudding 39
Cheese Puffs . . 39
Cheese Souffle 39
Eggs à la Martin . 37
Egg Puffs . . 37
Orange Omelet 38
Welsh Rarebit 38

MEATS, ENTREES.

Canapes, Lorenzo 48
Calf's Head, Scalloped 47
Calf's Heart, Stuffed 47
Chicken, To Cook Spring . . . 50
Chicken, Boiled 50
Chicken, Filling for 50
Chicken, Jellied 59
Chicken, Jellied 58
Chicken Livers 47
Chicken for Lunch 56
Chicken with Jelly, Minced . . 58
Chicken Terrapin 56
Chicken Croquettes 54
Croquettes 55
Croquettes 55
Croquettes (Meat and Hominy) . 55
Croquettes, Sweet Potato . . . 56

Chops à la Maintenon 48
Corn Beef 49
Devilled Dressing 57
Dutch Pudding 51
Frizzled Beef 51
Frogs' Legs, No. 1 58
Frogs' Legs, No. 2 58
Hamburg Steaks 51
Hash 52
Hash, Baked 52
Hash, Liver 52
Hash, Turkey 52
Kidney, Stewed 53
Liver, Pate of 46
Liver, Roast Calf's. . 45
Liver, Roast Spiced 46
Marrow on Toast 57
Mutton Cutlets à la Maintenon . . 48
Quail, Roast 45
Rissolles 54
Sweetbreads 53
Sweetbreads, Baked 53
Terrapin, to Dress 56
Terrapin, Chicken 56
Terrapin, Mock 57
Turkey Roast 45
Veal Cutlets, To Cook 49
Veal, Jellied 59
Veal Loaf 60
White Puddings 50

PORK.

Bacon—Receipt for Curing . . 67
Cheese Souse 68
Cheese Souse, To Make 68
Cure Hams, To 66
Curing Hams, Receipt for . . . 65
Curing Hams 66
Ham, To Boil and Bake a . . 69

Ham Patties	70	Egg Sandwiches	90
Pudding	69	Lemon Sandwiches	90
Roast Pig	69	Meat Sandwiches	90
		Olive Sandwiches	91

VEGETABLES

Apples, Fried	78		
Asparagus with Eggs	82	**DESSERTS.**	
Cauliflower, Escaloped	80	Apple Compote	108
Celery au Jus	81	Apple Dumplings, Baked	105
Cold Slaw	82	Apple Fritters	116
Cold Slaw	82	Apple Pie	117
Corn Pudding	79	Apple Pudding, Fancy	106
Corn Pudding	79	Bananas, Fried	116
Cornlet, Scalloped	80	Blanc Mange	111
Egg Plant, Stuffed	81	Blanc Mange	111
Frijoles	76	Blanc Mange, Chocolate	112
Macaroni	79	Blanc Mange, Cream	111
Mushrooms	78	Blueberry Pudding	107
Okra	76	Boiled Pudding, Old Fashioned	108
Potatoes au Gratin	77	Bread Pudding	106
Potatoes, Glazed Sweet	79	Bread and Apple Pudding	106
Potatoes, Lyonnaise	76	Cafe Parfait	98
Potatoes, Stewed	77	Charlotte Russe	112
Potatoes, Stuffed	77	Charlotte Russe	113
Rice	75	Charlotte Russe, Invalid's	113
Rice, To Boil	75	Cocoanut Pudding	104
Squash, To Cook Summer	78	Cream, Mrs. Shipman's	112
Tomatoes, Broiled	80	Cream, Velvet	112
		Cream Tapioca Pudding	104
SALADS, SALAD DRESSINGS &		Custard, Baked	102
SANDWICHES.		Custard, Boiled	115
French Dressing	88	Custard, Caramel	102
French Dressing	88	Custard Soufflé	102
Mayonnaise Dressing	88	Danish Pudding	103
Mayonnaise Dressing	89	Fig Pudding	101
Salad Dressing, Cooked	88	Frozen Peaches	98
Tartar Sauce	89	Frozen Strawberries	98
Tomato Jelly	87	Fruit Fritters, Batter for	116
Tomatoes Stuffed with Sweetbreads	87	Ginger Pudding	103
		Huckleberry Pudding	107

INDEX.

Ice Cream, Filling for Rich.	97
Ice Cream, Macaroon.	98
Ice Cream, Vanilla	97
Iced Rice Pudding with Compote of Oranges.	99
Imperial Pudding	99
Indian Pudding.	105
Indian Pudding, Boiled	108
Jelly, Boiled Wine	110
Jelly, Coffee	110
Jelly from Feet, To make	109
Jelly, Wine	110
Jellied Prunes	110
Lemon Pie.	118
Meringue	115
Mince Meat	117
Mince Meat	117
Oatmeal Pudding	105
Orange Ice	99
Peach Pudding	107
Peach Sponge	114
Plum Pudding	100
Plum Pudding	101
Prune Pudding	104
Pumpkin Pie	117
Putnam Thanksgiving Pudding, The	103
Rice Meringue Pudding	114
Rolly Poly Pudding	107
Strawberry Charlotte	114
Strawberry Meringue	114
Strawberry Short Cake	113
Transparent Pies	118
Transparent Puddings	119
Tylers	118
Washington Pie	119

SAUCES.

For Fish.

Cucumber Sauce	125
White Sauce	125

For Meats.

Brown Sauce	126
Chives Sauce	126
Lemon Sauce for Boiled Fowl	126
Papilotte Sauce	127

For Vegetables.

Cream or White Sauce	127
White Sauce	128
White Sauce or Drawn Butter	127

For Desserts.

Cream Sauce	129
Creamy Sauce	129
Devonshire Cream	128
Foamy Sauce	129
Hard Sauce	131
Hot Chocolate Sauce	131
Lemon Sauce	130
Sauce for Plum Pudding	130
Wine Sauce for Plum Pudding	129
Wine Sauce	130
Wine Sauce	130

CAKE.

Angel Food	139
Black Cake, To make	141
Boiled Icing	146
Caramel Cake	144
Chocolate Cake	145
Chocolate Icing	148
Cocoanut Drop Cakes	151
Cookies	149
Corn Starch Cake	139
Cream Drop Cakes	151
Cup Cake	139
Doughnuts	152
Drop Cakes	151
Drop Ginger Cakes	151
Feather Cake	139
Fruit Cake	141

INDEX.

Fruit Cake	141	Chocolate		158
Fruit Cake	142	Chocolate		158
Fruit Cake	142	Chocolate, To Prepare		159
Fruit Cake	142	Coffee, Mixture of		157
Gen. Lee Cake	140	Coffee, Boiled		157
Ginger Bread, Soft	148	Coffee, Filtered		158
Ginger Bread, Soft	149	Coffee, French		157
Ginger Bread, Soft	148	Champagne Cup		163
Ginger Cake, Soft	148	Cherry Cordial		163
Hickory Nut Macaroons	152	Cider Cup		162
Indian Meal Cake	140	Cider Cup		163
Instantaneous Frosting	147	Claret Cup		163
Jumbles	149	Egg Nogg		160
Lemon Jelly Cake	146	Egg Nogg		161
Lady Cake	138	Egg Nogg		161
Lunch Cake	137	Egg Nogg		161
Maple Sugar Icing	146	Ginger Beer		164
Marshmallow Filling	147	Hock Cup		161
Mocha Cake, No. 1	143	Hock Cup		163
Mocha Cake, No. 2	143	Lemonade, Indian		159
Nut Cakes	152	Mint Julep		163
Orange Cake	144	Mansion House Loving Cup		159
Orange Filling	147	Mulled Wine		162
Pistachio Cake	140	Mulled Wine		162
Plain Cake	145	Philadelphia Fish House Punch		159
Plain Cake	145	Punch		159
Plain Cake	146	Tea		158
Plain Icing	147	Tea, Iced		158
Sand Tarts	150	Tea Punch		160
Sugar Cakes	150	**PRESERVES AND PICKLES.**		
Sugar Cakes	150	Brandied Peaches		171
Sponge Cake	138	Brandied Peaches		171
Sponge Cake	138	Cantaloupe, Sweet Pickled		174
Suggestions on Cake Baking	137	Chili Sauce		175
Taylor Cakes	150	Conserves		169
BEVERAGES.		Cucumber Pickle		172
Apple Tod	160	Currants, Spiced		171
Apple Toddy	160	Currant Jelly		169
Blackberry Wine	164	Ginger Pears		171

INDEX.

Green Tomato Pickle 172
Mangoe Pickles 173
Martina Pickles 173
Orange Marmalade 170
Oysters, Pickled 175
Pear Butter 170
Quince Jelly 169
Strawberries, To Preserve . . . 170
Sweet Pickle 174
Tomato Catsup 175
Tomato Sauce 176
Walnut Pickles 173
Watermelon Pickle 174

CANDY.
Almond Candy 182
Chocolate Caramels 181
Chocolate Caramels 181
Chocolate Caramels 181
Cocoanut Bars 183
Everton Taffy 182
Marshmallows 183
Peanut Taffy 182
Taffy 182
Taffy, White 182
Toffee 183

MISCELLANEOUS.
Abbreviations VI
Ants, To Drive Away 195
Benzine Cleaning Fluid . . . 190
Black Lace and Net, To Wash . 195
Brass, To Clean 198
Calico, To Set the Colors in . . 194
Carpets and Woolens, To Clean . 191
Chapped Hands, For 189
Cleaning Compound 190
Cleaning Fluid 191

Cologne, To Make 189
Covers Off Fruit Jars, To Take . 197
Eggs Until Winter, To Keep . . 196
Equivalents of Weights in Measure VII
Flannel, To Wash 194
Flowers Fresh, To Keep . . . 197
Furniture Bright, Keeping . . . 196
Gilt, To Take Spots Off 198
Grease Out of Carpets, To Take . 195
Indelible Ink, Marking With . . 196
Ink, To Take Out 193
Ink, Out of Carpets, To Take . 195
Lye, To Make 192
Matting, To Take Spots Out of . 195
Mildew, To Take Out . . . 190
Mildew, To Remove 190
Mould on Preserves, To Prevent 197
Mutton Suet, To Render . . . 193
Pot-Pourri 189
Prints or Engravings, To Clean . 196
Rust from Knives or any Steel, To Remove 197
Silver Polish 197
Soap, To Make Hard 192
Soap, To Make Soft 192
Tins, To Clean 198
Velvet, How to Steam . . . 190
Wall Paper, English Receipt for Cleaning 191
White Clothes, To Take Stains Out of 193
White Paint, To Clean 193
White Marble Hearths, To Clean 195
White Marble Hearths, To Take Spots Out of 195

The First National Bank,

❦ ❦ ❦

Capital and Surplus. - - $1,250,000.

❦ ❦ ❦

Corner Fifth Avenue and Wood Street.

❦ ❦ ❦

Charles E. Speer, F. H. Skelding,
PRESIDENT. CASHIER.

Alex. Nimick, Robt. D. Book,
VICE PRESIDENT. ASST. CASHIER.

❦ ❦ ❦

LOCATED right in the heart of the shopping district, with a dozen lines of cars passing the door, and reaching every suburb of both cities.

Ladies will find this one of the most conveniently located banks in the city for the transaction of business.

Home and shopping accounts will receive prompt attention as well as those of firms and corporations.

J. Painter & Sons Co.

BOSTON.   CHICAGO.

ESTABLISHED 1859.

Howe, Brown & Company, Limited,

MANUFACTURERS OF

FINE STEEL.

HOWE'S TOOL STEEL.

HOWE'S SPECIAL TOOL STEEL.

HOWE'S CRUCIBLE CAST SPRING STEEL.

CRUCIBLE AND OPEN HEARTH STEEL
    OF ALL DESCRIPTIONS.

POLISHED DRILL RODS.

OFFICE AND WORKS

Penn Avenue and Seventeenth Street,

PITTSBURG, PA.

Use Our Quaker Cabinet.

Enjoy **Turkish, Russian, Sulphur, Perfumed, Thermal, Medicated and Vapor Baths** in the privacy of your room at home or abroad for **three cents. Water Baths cleanse the outer skin or surface only.** Makes your blood pure, your sleep sound, your skin soft, white and beautiful. You feel younger, like a new being. Ladies are enthusiastic in its praise. No assistant or experience needed. A child can operate it.

DESCRIPTION.—Weight, 5 lbs. Best made. Germ-proof and water-proof lined. Odorless, antiseptic, hygienic cloth extended by a coppered steel frame. Patented. Size, folded, 15 in. square, 3 in. thick. Easily carried. **Price,** complete, including heater, valuable formulas, directions, etc., **$5.00.** Every Quaker Cabinet is guaranteed by us to do the work and be exactly as represented, or money refunded.

It Produces Cleanliness, Health, Strength and a Beautiful Complexion.

Dispels Colds, Fevers, Skin Diseases and Eruptions, Cures Rheumatism, Sciatica, Obesity, Neuralgia, Bronchitis, Quinsy, Eczema, La Grippe, Malaria, Catarrh, Headaches, Female Complaints, Pneumonia, Piles, Dropsy and all Blood, Skin, Nerve and Kidney Troubles.

A Hot Springs at Home.

J. T. McKENNAN,

Druggist and Apothecary,   431 MARKET ST., PITTSBURG, PA.

W. G. SCHIRMER, Manager.

Reserved.

GEO. K. STEVENSON & CO.,
GROCERS.

We have a tempting array of good things at tempting prices. We particularly invite all who are not familiar with our stores, to visit either or both, and see how attractive food stores can be made.

We have always felt that a Grocery Store should be made inviting, and have endeavored to make ours so, not only in the display of fine goods, but in prices as well.

GEO. K. STEVENSON & CO.,

TWO STORES: { Sixth Ave., opp. Trinity Church, Centre and Highland Aves., E. E.,

PITTSBURG, PA.

REYMER & BROTHERS,

508-512 Wood Street,

Manufacturers of the Finest and Choicest Confectionery.

To send a box of "Reymer's Best" to your friends would be a rare treat indeed, and no doubt highly appreciated. There are many would be imitators, but it is not Reymer's. It may be merely a matter of taste to some, but to taste "Reymer's Best" you will at once admit it cannot be surpassed in richness of flavors and fine material.

Special attention given to Luncheon and Dinner Candies, of which we make a fine variety—Hats, Baskets, Rings, Bow Knots, Zig Zags and other novelties.

Orders will receive special attention and prompt delivery.

REYMER'S.

The Siegfried Pharmacy,

Corner Highland and Centre Avenues,

Telephone, 800 E. E.

❧ ❧ ❧

The execution of Prescription Work *and the compounding of Family receipts* Our Specialty.

We carry also a full line of Physicians' Supplies and Surgical Dressings, Bandages, Lints, Gauzes, Cottons, Ligatures, etc.

Every requisite for the toilet and sick-room.

Reymer's Fine Confections.

Pure Soda Water.

Syrups being made by us from the fresh fruit.

Reserved.

JOS. HORNE & CO.

Housefurnishings.

We have always paid a great deal of attention to this Department.

We put it in the basement, simply because there is abundance of room down there, and that is what a department of that kind needs.

You will find anything and everything in the way of Household Articles.

Any new invention for making labor throughout the house easy makes its way very quickly to this Department, and you will always find the new devices, as well as the old, waiting for you.

It is, perhaps, the most complete Housefurnishing Department in the State.

Penn Avenue and Fifth Street.

LOUIS SCHULENBERG.   J. WILLIAM PORTS.

SCHULENBERG & PORTS,

Riding, Livery and Boarding Stables,

BELLEFONTE ST. AND FIFTH AVE.

GOOD SADDLE, DRIVING AND COMBINATION HORSES
ALWAYS ON HAND FOR SALE. ALSO, HORSES
SOLD ON COMMISSION.

Instruction in Riding and Driving given by

Telephone, CHARLES A. BISHOP,
Bellefield 266. LOUIS SCHULENBERG.

JUNIATA IRON WORK.
ESTABLISHED 1824.
Shoenberger Steel Co.

Manufacturers of

Pig Metal,
Open Hearth and Bessemer Steel,
Sheets, Blooms, Slabs and Billets.
Fire Box, Boiler and Tank Steel Plates,

Iron and Steel Horse and Mule Shoes,
Horse Shoe Bar, Toe Calks,
Skelp, Tin Plate Bar and Sheet Iron.

J. L. D. SPEER & CO.

BANKERS,

First National Bank Building,
255 Fifth Avenue,   Pittsburg, Pa.

HIGH GRADE BONDS FOR SAVINGS BANKS AND
PRIVATE INVESTORS.

MEMBERS OF PITTSBURG STOCK EXCHANGE.

ASSOCIATE OFFICES:

Members of New York Stock Exchange.

Members of Philadelphia Stock Exchange.

Members of Baltimore Stock Exchange.

Business Paper Discounted
and
Loans made on
Collateral.

Long Distance Telephone,
Pittsburg 2229.

Established 1840.

J. C. GROGAN,
Jeweler,

Diamonds, Rubies, Sapphires and Pearls.

RARE SPECIMENS IN FANCY GEMS.

Experience and close study of setting Jewels, including finest workmanship, places my stock amongst the first in this country.

The Grogan Watch.

When you are interested in the purchase of a reliable timepiece, don't fail to consider my stock. Comprises every variety. All guaranteed.

STERLING SILVER DINING SERVICES.

Complete outfits that match perfectly. Shapes and styles not surpassed in any market. The variety in odd single pieces for appropriate gifts can not be described in this space.

TABLE CUTLERY.   **SILVER MOUNTED LEATHER GOODS.**

HALL CLOCKS.
SOLE AGENT FOR THE TUBULAR CHIME.

PRIZE CUPS.

The variety collected together this season surpasses any ever brought to this city.

J. C. GROGAN,
443 MARKET ST., COR. FIFTH AVE.   PITTSBURG, PA.

Pittsburgh Bank for Savings,——

210 Fourth Avenue.

❧ ❧ ❧

Assets over $3,400,000.

❧ ❧ ❧

Four Per Cent. Interest on Time Deposits.

❧ ❧ ❧

Your Account Solicited.

Ladies are guaranteed prompt and courteous treatment.

James S. Kuhn, President.

Wm. J. Jones, Treasurer.

Reserved.

Jos. Loughrey & Son,

MANUFACTURERS AND DEALERS IN

Harness, Saddles, Bridles,

Blankets, Robes, Collars, Whips,

Trunks, Satchels and

Travelers' Outfits, ♦ ♦ ♦ ♦

438 Wood Street,

TELEPHONE 114.   PITTSBURG, PA.

Jos. Eichbaum & Co.,

Printers, Stationers,

Steel and Copper Plate Engravers and Printers,

Fancy Goods,

Artists' Materials,

242 FIFTH AVENUE,   PITTSBURG, PA.

JOHN T. WRITT,
Practical Caterer,

7225 Susquehanna Street,　　　East End,
and 209 Fourth Avenue,
Room 4.　　　　　　Pittsburg, Pa.
'PHONE, PGH. 358.

WE HAVE NO RESTAURANT OR STALE FOOD. NOTHING KEPT OVER OR TAKEN BACK FROM YOUR RESIDENCE.

We are prepared to furnish Weddings, Suppers, Parties, Luncheons, Teas, Banquets, etc.

We are near the market; everything is fresh cooked, delivered and served to order.

We make a specialty of Salads, Timbals, Croquets and Pattie Filling of all kinds.

We are well known in Allegheny and the East End. And can refer you to many ladies in both cities.

Respectfully,
JOHN T. WRITT.

GREENHOUSES,　　　　　　　　　　MARKET STAND,
Boggs Ave., Mt. Washington.　　　　　No. 181 Allegheny.

A. W. SMITH,
Florist,

339 SIXTH AVENUE.　　　　　　　　PITTSBURG, PA.

> BEAUTIFUL PLANTS. . . . .
> CHOICE FRESH FLOWERS. . .
> ARTISTIC FLORAL AND PLANT DECORATIONS. . . . .

A. W. SMITH,
Telephone 2280.　　　　　　　　　339 Sixth Avenue.

SOCIAL
EVENTS,

RECEPTIONS and Theatre Parties desiring high-class livery service, will find our equipment eminently satisfactory.

OUR Park Traps, Carriages and Broughams, being of the newest designs and most approved pattern, and with our careful liveried drivers, give the style and finish of the best of private turnouts.

EXCELLENT CARE AND ATTENTION GIVEN TO BOARDING HORSES.

RIDING AND DRIVING TAUGHT.

Schenley Riding Academy,

'Phone, Bellefield 172.   BAYARD AND NEVILLE STS.

In Medicine and
In Food

You want the ingredients fresh and pure. With two up-to-date stores in excellent locations, our advantages for handling pure and fresh drugs are unexcelled.

Our candies are the best we can buy; Reymer's, Lowney's, Hershey's and Allegretti's.

True fruit juices and distilled water used in our Soda Water.

IMPORTED AND DOMESTIC CIGARS.

KAERCHER DRUG CO.

62 Federal St., Allegheny, Pa.   4701 Fifth Ave., cor. Neville, Pittsburg, Pa.
ALLEGHENY, 4.   (TELEPHONES)   BELLEFIELD, 208.

T. Reed McKnight,

Gas, Electric and Combination Fixtures.

Finest Display between
New York and Chicago.

Third Floor—Take Elevator.

Standard Building,
531 Wood Street.

PERFECT CATERING.
PERFECT PASTRY.
PERFECT ICES.
PERFECT ICE CREAMS.
PERFECT SWEETMEATS.

W. R. Kuhn & Co.
E. E.

Tel. 158
679
6202 Penn Avenue.

Every Woman is Interested
in the furnishing of the Bath Room.

"Standard" Bath Tubs and Plumbing Fixtures are unequaled in beauty, strength and durability.

All parts are exposed and easily accessible.

The various articles can be finished to match or harmonize with the surroundings and all details are carefully considered.

"S. M. Co." is cast on the bottom of every Bath, affording protection against the substitution of inferior goods.

STANDARD MANUFACTURING CO.

Catalogue on Application.   Pittsburg, Pa.

KNOX SAILOR HATS.

* * * *

The established superiority of Knox Hats was never more marked than it is this season.

The new sailor is a marvel of stylish elegance.

Smooth Braids, $5.00
Rough Braids, .   . 4.00
The New Jumbo Braid, 4.00

Knox Sailors are sold in Pittsburg only by us. None is genuine without the Knox trade mark.

Paulson Sailors, similar to the Knox in shape, $2.50 and $3.00.

Splendid display of Trimmed Millinery and Walking Hats.

PAULSON BROS.
441 WOOD STREET.

Reserved.

J. R. WELDIN & CO.,

429-431 Wood Street,
PITTSBURG, PA.

ENGRAVERS OF ———

Calling Cards.
Invitations to Teas,
Receptions, Dances,
Banquets and Weddings,
Monograms, Addresses,
Crests and Coats of Arms.

MAKERS OF ———

Table Cards, Dance Programs,
Menus and Fine Papers for
Polite Correspondence. . . .

ALL THE LATEST EASTERN IDEAS.

CARL A. WUNDERLY.   AUGUST WUNDERLY.

WUNDERLY BROS.,
ART STORE.

Etchings, Engravings, Water Colors and Oil Paintings, Picture Frames and Mirrors.

Regilding Frames, Repairing and Renovating a Specialty.

No. 329 Sixth Avenue,

Next to Duquesne Club.   PITTSBURG, PA.

Fine Flowers.   Artistic Decorations.

Randolph & McClements,

Floral Experts.

Tel., E. E. 25.   South Highland Ave.
Residence, E. E. 616.   and Baum St., E. E.

BUY HAINES' TRUNKS

GEO. S. HAINES CO.,

SOLE MANUFACTURER,

No. 528 Wood Street, PITTSBURG.

Positively no Agents or Branch Stores in Either City.

GOLF SHOES   *For Ladies and Gentlemen*

... AT CAIN'S.

And do not forget we are NOT on the Corner now.

Our Number is 503 MARKET STREET.

A BOOM TO EAST END!

THE C. H. ROWE CO.

Cor. Penn and Highland Aves.

A long-felt want is at last filled. Everything a well-dressed man or woman may need will be found in our spacious store rooms.

"COME, SHOP WITH US."

All Car Lines pass the Door.

"If you cannot find it here, there's no use looking elsewher

UPHOLSTERY EFFECTIVENESS

Many Draperies and Hangings are put in place that entirely wanting in effect—that do not lend the apartm the air of comfort and beauty sought for.

HAVE THEM RIGHT.

See our New and Stylish Decorative Fabrics, and let us send an experienced man to give you estimates and show you designs—Modern Designs, that produce the charm that rich hangings should give.

E. GROETZINGER,

CARPETINGS AND
DRAPERIES. . .

627=629 Penn Avenue.

www.ingramcontent.com/pod-product-compliance
Lightning Source LLC
Chambersburg PA
CBHW021807230426
43669CB00008B/655